**Plague
Songs**

Plague
Songs

Martin Rowson

Smoke
STACK
BOOKS

Smokestack Books
1 Lake Terrace, Grewelthorpe, Ripon HG4 3BU
e-mail: info@smokestack-books.co.uk
www.smokestack-books.co.uk

ISBN 9781916312173

Smokestack Books
is represented
by Inpress Ltd

For Jon Medlam
and for Alison Brown,
in loving memory of both.

And for Luke,
without whom
none of this, etc...

And, as ever
and with all my love,
for Anna, Fred and Rose.

Contents

Foreword

On Friday 3 January 2020, having filed my cartoon for the next day's *Guardian* early (it portrayed Donald Trump pissing fire onto Iran) I made the twenty-minute train journey from Lewisham to Charing Cross and then walked through Central London to Soho to take some photos of Greek Street on my phone, as research for a commission.

On Thursday 16 January 2020 I went to the launch of my friend Carol Isaacs' brilliant graphic memoir *The Wolf of Baghdad,* held at London's Cartoon Museum. I'd been feeling a bit odd – a tad fluey – for a couple of days, but didn't think much of it. To help me self-medicate, the Museum's Alison Brown plied me with cocktails she'd devised specially to theme with Carol's book. I left early, feeling achier and achier, and when my wife Anna got home from her evening seminar, she found me shivering and huddled in the kitchen with a temperature of over 100.

For the next two weeks I was incapable of anything, feeling iller than I had for fifty years. Too enervated and exhausted even to draw, I slept most of the time, in between drenching night sweats, claustrophobic bouts of breathlessness and aching eyes and joints, my sense of taste not gone but twisted, so I felt enveloped in a headily sulphurous and slightly faecal miasma. I didn't imagine for a second I could possibly be suffering from the disease in China increasingly dominating the news.

But I was. An antibody test six months later proved the fact. I'd caught it simply by catching a train and then walking through the streets of Central London in early January, a fact my late father, a virologist, would have relished. Almost exactly a year later, following unconnected surgery, wonderful, lovely, funny, brilliant Alison Brown died of it, like thousands and thousands of others before her.

On 23 March 2020, the British Government belatedly announced a full national Lockdown, although by then most people were stopping indoors of their own volition. On my last journey into Central London to stock up on art supplies, I was reminded of the fragmentary Anglo-Saxon poem 'The Ruin', in which the narrator wanders through the abandoned ruins of a Roman city. I gave a *Big Issue* seller a fiver but told him to keep the magazine and sell it to someone else. My mind was on infectivity rather than philanthropy.

A few days earlier my friend the poet Luke Wright had commenced on a programme of 100 nightly half-hour poetry readings on Twitter. I'd met Luke four years previously at the Laugharne Weekend in Wales, when he picked me up in a hotel bar. We rapidly established weird affinities, like being adopted, our adoptive fathers sharing an identical hobby, both of our little fingers being bent, having similar tastes and enthusiasms and much else besides. Indeed, I often suspect that we're both failed prototypes constructed by some shadowy and sinister intelligence, cack-handedly seeking to create the ultimate Bumptious Gobshite committed to strenuously avoiding ever getting a proper job. I'm not sure that Luke agrees with this analysis. Either way, we've done quite a few poetry gigs together and I've illustrated one of his books.

By early May his daily Twitter gigs were beginning to take their toll. I'd check in on them fairly regularly, and Luke was looking increasingly jaded and haggard. I proposed, therefore, a project to lift him from his languorous torpor, in which we would each write a daily poem just for shits and giggles. We should do it, moreover, on the Cartier-Bresson model, in honour of the great French photographer who only ever took one exposure of a subject: in other words, I wanted us to just knock the bastards out fast, forego agonising revision in pursuit of elusive perfection and move on, thus keeping our minds fresh and nimble in those dark days of high Spring in this foul and deadly year. Luke agreed, and naturally enough produced a couple of poems, moaned a lot and then scarpered (though in fairness it should be mentioned in mitigation he was also homeschooling his two young sons throughout).

I, however, persisted. From 11 May to 26 November more or less every day (saving most weekends and most of a snatched week in the Scottish Highlands in September) I sat down first thing after breakfast and wrote a poem, although later on five were written, as in The Olden Days, on trains. Whereas many found their lockdown solace in sourdough baking or growing beards, I was soon drawing mine from this regular matutinal mental throat clearing. Some of the poems reacted directly to the cataclysm unfolding in the empty streets around me; others riffed on the latest political catastrophes of the day; some were old ideas I finally had time and discipline to beat into vague poetic shape; others yet were random thoughts or lines or sometimes just a word or two that flashed through my mind in the shower or while I was shaving or even in a dream, which I'd then lasso and let drag me across the scrub to see where the hell we were going to end up. Many are furious, some are meant to be funny; quite a lot, I hope, are both. And an awful lot, unavoidably, are about Death – not least that of my beloved and very old friend Jon Medlam, who died of lung cancer in August. After six and a half months, in the same way they'd started, the poems then stopped.

What follows, therefore, is almost all of those daily poems, in the order in which they were written. My publisher and editor Andy Croft decided to omit about four, as they didn't quite fit. I dropped one (a passionate if ironical plea to Boycott *The Guardian*) as it works when shouted out loud to a bunch of drunks at a gig, but withers and dies on the page. Andy and I have otherwise changed practically nothing, apart from the occasional metrical or verbal infelicity which subsequently niggled. On average, these things would take up an hour of my morning as I clubbed them into shape, though in one or two cases a lot longer, and in others hardly any time at all. If you want to read the unedited versions, you can find them on my website www. martinrowson.com, published the day they were written, raw as a grazed shin.

This was also the state they were in when I'd email them each day to a small group of people who I'd like to thank now for their forbearance and more generally. They were: Andy Croft, Luke Wright, my agent Matthew Marland, my webmeister Rich Hobbs, Mike Quille, Jon Tregenna, the trespasser and illustrator Nick Hayes and my ever vigilant factotum Patricia Bargh. Andy, in addition to publishing this book, also ran a couple in *The Morning Star*. Mike ran many more on his excellent Culture

Matters website. Rich posted them on my website every day. And Jon, rather wonderfully, has put 52 of them to music, across three *Plague Songs* albums, performed by a wealth of talent and available to buy as a CD and view on YouTube. Patricia said she enjoyed a lot of them and Luke offered occasional advice, little of which I heeded. Although I did establish that, despite being a professional poet of some standing who even teaches other aspiring poets, he'd never previously heard of Yeats' 'The Second Coming'. Like they say, every day's a school day.

And there you have it, and all that's left to me is to throw my darlings at your feet, and you'll either pick them up and cuddle them or stamp on the squirming sods. But whatever their fate now, this is a genuine daily response to a unique and terrible period in all our lives, in which thousands upon thousands of our fellow citizens died and a small number of our nation's governing party's chums made millions.

Martin Rowson
Lewisham, 21 January 2021

The Enemy Within:
A Paranoid Round in a Time of Pestilence

Each time I cough
To clear my throat
I wonder what
This might denote

And then my thoughts
Start going viral
In an endless
Downwards spiral:

That cough is
Obviously Corona!
I'm harbouring
An inner Jonah

To shipwreck me!
A tracheal traitor
Who'll haul me
To the ventilator!

Inflaming my
Raw alveoli
Into swollen
Ravioli

And every rattling
Gob of phlegm's
Shortcutting me
To lonely crems

So fast the fucker's
Gone ballistic
To fit me up
As a statistic!

My airways block!
Air can't get through!
I'll isolate
To ICU...

Then I calm down.
The airways clear;
My breathlessness
Was just my fear;

I don't yet need
An autopsy;
We're all in this
And not just me!

And then I cough
To clear my throat...

3 April 2020

Anchorites

Now listen. So this wanker, right,
Says 'You must all be anchorites!
Stay in! Watch 'Casablanca', right?
Or you'll all die point blank!' Oh right!

So we all became anchorites,
In our own Lubyankas, right?
Observing our own danker rites
To help outsmart this canker, right?
Like thresholding clapped thanks. Yeah, right.

Then, when we'd all been anchorites
Once more he jawed, this wanker, right?
And drawled, 'My favourite crank, all right,
Says you're all thick as planks! Ah, right!
And now you must all hanker, right,
For freedom! So up-anchor! Right!'

He didn't add that bankers' right
To growing assets shrank all right
The longer we were anchorites.
But Wealth will Death outrank! Yeah! Right!
They need their bleeding shanks, all right?
So when the cell door clanks, all right,
The outside world's the tank! Oh. Right.

And so we all stayed anchorites
Inside or out. It stank all right,
But try and get your rancour right
And dream how we'll outflank the right
Once we're massed ranks of anchorites,
Our hanks of hair all lank, all right,
Once we amass as anchorites,
A mass of anchorites. Yeah, right.
A mass of anchorites.

11 May 2020

Following the Science

I'm following the Science!
Like a lost but trusting waif
I'm chasing after wisdom
And a promise I'll be safe.

I'm following the Science
For its methodology
Will manufacture better worlds
Just made for you and me

As I'm following the Science
Right across the bright green fields
Left unbereft by insect deaths
And with new five fold yields

And I'm following the Science
As it leads me through the woods,
Through thickets of appliances
And dumped consumer goods

Then I'm following the Science
Though I don't know what it means
When it hurries me past clearings full
Of gods caught in machines

Still, I'm following the Science,
Past jarred body parts in brine,
Caught up in roots with some pursuits
Of Dr Frankenstein's

And I'm following the Science
Straight past Cottontail & Flopsy
And Peter Rabbit in a cage
Awaiting an autopsy

And I'm following the Science
Which now decks me with a halter
To lead me through the deep dark wood
To a thing built like an altar

Then I'm following the Science
Deeper in, and on we race,
And the Science hands me callipers
For measuring my face

And I'm following the Science
To see how you can be me
Through the science of eugenics
With a can of Zyklon B

And I'm following the Science
As we fall down a black hole
To the bottom where a boffin
Is now genemapping my soul

Til I'm following the Science
To the surface, with aplomb,
To emerge deep in a desert
Where it's built an atom bomb

Then I'm following the Science
With Apollo! Riding pillion
I'll trawl his halls for carbon spoils
At 500 parts per million

And I'm following the Science!
Though by now I'm double-blinded
So I can't see its complicity
In the crimes that humankind did

Through following the Science,
Nor the planet that we've wanked on,
For the Science seldom makes it clear
That we're no more than plankton

And following the Science
While tugging at our cocks
Has merely helped to bind us
To Prometheus's rocks.

So sure, follow the Science,
But calculate the odds.
Scientists are human too,
And Heaven has no Gods.

12 May 2020

Herd Immunity

When they come to write the epics
Of these dark times, will a prefix
      By a future critic opine 'Woe is me!'
Showing how the poets fudged
Their duty as they nudged
      Us all to roam through realms of poesy?

And will each gruesome saga
Drive its tearful readers gaga
      As it adumbrates the politicians' crimes?
And shall each mournful sonnet
Have the Mark of Cain upon it
      Through the simple absences of some true rhymes?

For the poetical lever
That we need to lift this fever
      Needs bards! Proclaiming rhymes! In echoing halls!
For while I guess I'm like you
And I'll tolerate a haiku
      In grim times verse sans rhymes is utter balls.

Nor will some weedy loner
Serve in just rhyming 'Corona'
      With 'donor', 'boner', 'stoner'; nor inspire us,
And our victory will be pyrrhical
If we've limited The Lyrical
      By copping out and singing of 'The Virus'.

True, its name's 'Covid-19'
And a poetry machine
      Might just wrangle that last number into verse
Though verses arithmetical
Are cruelly antithetical
      To poetry and make the whole thing worse.

Nor does 'Ovid isn't bovvered'
Nor 'Livid' have it covered;
      Leave assonance to asses like Luke Wright
We need 'COVID's' one true rhyme
To distinguish us from slime
      And set our yearning human souls alight!

But the one true rhyme for 'Covid'
Is – unfortunately – 'Bovid';
      That is, pertaining to or just like cattle,
And in this foul Pandemic
We need something more anthemic
      Than mooing to our deaths in this great battle.

So leave your escritoire
And abjure the abattoir!
        Plato was right, as every schoolboy knows!
Eschew verse, my dear old mucker!
We'll obliterate this fucker
        By addressing the repulsive cunt in prose!

13 May 2020

Haute Couture (in the High Style)

The husks of harvested cocoons
    Lie strewn across the salon floor
        Like skulls from a late 14th century Asiatic battle;

The zinc baths bristle, acidically
    drizzling dissolving gristle into vats
        to liberate the trim from taints of flesh
And knurled thimbles, prized,
    Are prised from pricking thumbs to roll
        Quite unsurprisingly beneath the plan chest
           in the corner.

They fall from hands whose spans
    Have spun the looms to stretch the thread
        Towards the invisibility of spiders' silk
           And as inescapably, webbily, envelopingly
           sticky as a swab.

And the stitching is exquisite.
    The patterns in the plan chest, chalked templates
        Covering greasy tracing paper & pinpricked to a bruise,
He cuts a different way.
But the stitching is exquisite,
    Warp and wefting through the billions of junctions,
        Just snagging for a second on the pointillistic air
           Then double stitching through each brace of
           lungs, then to the next
In blurs of movement sleeker than machines.

He leans back, half admires the cut,
    Glances at her sleeping, listless, sad,
        Eczema'd by human greed and folly.
Then he drapes the garment, intangible as dreams
        And gossamer as an escaping thought and sheer
            as a miniscus
Across her curving form.

Earth bridles, yawns, then shrugs.
    And then snuggles and rubs her warming Arctic
        Against his mushroom stubble.
'Oh darling!' purrs the planet,
    And hugging her Pandemic frock around her, smiles
        and coos, 'My clever virus! This is just divine!'

Elsewhere some low, unhappy creatures
    Farmed for fur and fury
        And non-consensually essential to High Fashion,
Continue coughing in their crates.

14 May 2020

Rainbows

Remember outside? Your government boasts it's victorious!

Rightly outraged? You get back indoors, viper!

Rubbish orator yelps greasily before inspiring violence

Reality obliges your granny be interred virtually.

Red Orange Yellow Green Blue Indigo Virus.

15 May 2020

Killer Matt

Harold Shipman down in hell looks up in envy;
In his Broadmore cell Pete Sutcliffe heaves a sigh,
For neither one could match
The speech and the despatch
Of KILLER MATT slapsticking who should die.

And Goering doffs his crown of deadly nightshade,
Holds it aloft and coos 'See if this fits!
Let's forget our wartime quarrels!
KILLER MATT deserves the laurels!
He's killed off more than I did in the Blitz!'

Killer Matt! Killer Matt!
He knocks into a cocked hat
The tales of murderers in days of yore!
Killer Matt! Killer Matt!
A machine-gun's rat-a-tat
On the Western Front could not kill any more!

It's killed your gran & grandad and their carers,
A super serial-killer, still at large
Whose Ambassadors of Death
Unaware killed with their breath
Untested when the poor souls were discharged!

Though uncowled, he's both grim & mediocre,
And has spread more plague than a Sumatran rat:
With his first in PPE
He lies to the BBC
And he'll get away with it, will KILLER MATT!

Killer Matt! Killer Matt!
Next he'll cross-infect your cat!
He's the Tory Party's Fred West! Killer Matt!
And nobody can smirk .
And make it look like such hard work
As can the King of Killers, Killer Matt!

Killer Matt! Killer Matt!
Is that drool on his cravat?
Does he now exude a heady graveyard smell?
But he'll get his just reward
When the murderers applaud
His inevitable homecoming in Hell.

16 May 2020

Witches

Growing older has its hitches
As the body suffers glitches
Til you think that every itch is
Proof you harbour inner snitches
Who'll grass you up to Death, whose stitches
Will bind your shroud before she ditches
You in the grave as black as pitch is,
And deadly duller than Ipswich is.

And so we all ape dumb ostriches;
Try to ignore all random twitches;
Say Life's so easy – like Quidditch is –
But all the while we hear the scritches
Of Death's nib... So embrace Life's riches
While you can! And yet, the bitch is
Growing older has its hitches
As the body suffers glitches...
But now my turds all float! Like witches!!

18 May 2020

Freedom

There's a bored baboon who's wanking on the bonnet of our car
In an empty precinct lined by closed up shops
And there is in his demeanour something telling us, thus far,
There's no real point in trying to call the cops.

Before he'd started wanking he had shat, & through it squirmed
Vile parasites that grinned & coiled like vipers
And his face did not reveal just what such things might have confirmed
As the baboon ripped off both our windscreen wipers.

An iron collar round his neck had worn a scarlet weal,
Rusty chains thread from it to a distant door
Where a short man's counting money that he stole from an appeal
Celebrities had got up for the poor.

He comes to climax. Christ! The beast's spunk stinks of stale iced buns!
He weeps – the poor thing's very highly strung.
He'd been dreaming about liberals being hunted down with guns,
Eugenics, vaccines, tax and Toby Young.

Then the baboon bares his yellow fangs & pimps his purple arse
And lifts a leg to copiously pee
In our faces, thankfully protected by the windscreen glass,
And all of us imagine that we're free.

There's a bored baboon still wanking on the bonnet of our car.
We stare at him and he stares back at us.
And neither of us thinks that things would not have got this far
If only we had thought to catch the bus.

19 May 2020

What Could Possibly Go Wrong
(Orca Sing Near Moorgate)

A deep sea diver jounces through Atlanta's sunken streets,
Their diving boots as heavy as regret.

A hedgerow grows up through a scree of hedgies' bones,
Piled, smashed, a full five fathoms' worth of air
Below a previous window.

It has long since crashed,
Just like the system,
Into ruins.

A fawn tip-toes on its tony hooves
Through leaf litters of derivatives.

Bats roost in a useless legislative chamber's
Few remaining rafters.

Orca sing near Moorgate.

But the tiny glimpses of a billion futures,
Fragile as flecks of fishfood floating in a tank of hungry tench
Are gone as soon as you awake,
Dog-tired,
To face another dreadful day
Farming triffids for their oil.

20 May 2020

Dirty Nasty Lockdown

Come on lads! What's wrong with Lock Down?
Perfect time to wind the clock down
We're kings now! Wear an ad hoc crown!
Beyond the gaze of coppers! Mock Down
Syndrome kiddies! Wear a frock! Drown
Stray cats in the pond! Sjambok brown
Bastards steal our jobs, then knock down
20 pints and get yer cock down
Yer best mate's throat, then get it pocked brown
Bumming all your pets!
Phwoar!
That's Lock Down!

20 May 2020

Pallbearers

Auntie Sarah's
Carer's
Pallbearers'
Nostrils flare as
They imperceptibly shift the weight on all four of them there.

And in a world that's been declared
As fit simply for billionaires
Don't fret you can't compare
Whether this or that is fair.
However clean the air is,
However loud the prayers
And however fixed the pallbearers'
Long, inscrutable stares,
It's invariably rare
That a shroud becomes its wearer.

21 May 2020

They've Cancelled Death

They cancelled Glasto, Wimbledon, the fete,
So now they've cancelled Death –
Though with the promise it'll be back here next year.

It seems it isn't safe.
That social distancing the teeming souls
Along the Styx's sepulchral banks won't wash.

And so a cos-play minister,
Another mediocre crank who's just short-strawed the presser,
Lies and squeals 'Another first for Britain!'

Ranks of caught reporters' heads,
Like bits and bobs some nutcase keeps in jars to sate his scientific interest,
Nod from the surrounding screens.

So they furloughed the plumed horses,
The gravediggers and morticians,
While the crematoria cooled.

And the sick get sicker
With no chances of a last blessed release,
Just stacked in artics spiralling round each town.

And irrespective of their recent callous flush,
The care homes become black holes of Calcutta,
A leafy streeted scandal now a tinderbox that never quite explodes.

And if some whining trolls in *The Spectator*
Demand their Right to Die as English Freedom's Bounty,
We all just check our phones

Then zoom Eternity
Connecting to the Great Beyond remotely
With a screenful of howling brown snowstorming static

And furtively check emails,
And maybe nod if some white noise grabs at something edging sense,
Paying no attention to the far-off comedy screams.

22 May 2020

LockJaw

What if, instead of Lockdown, we had lockjaw,
Some viral way to shut the fuckers up,
Those Tory trolls who think that, if they shock more,
This fills to brimming o'er life's joyful cup?

What if, to spread the lockjaw, we had locksmiths
To padlock all these wankers gob to arse?
Would we be spared the bastards' shit filled crocks if
We centipeded them & their whole class?

What if, on top of locksmiths, we had lockets
Containing pictures of those we hold dear
They wouldn't contain clowns in rich men's pockets.
I trust that I've now made the whole thing clear.

23 May 2020

Barbarians

The barbarians are not at the gates.
        They're through the gates.
             They built the gates,
Granting ingress through the walls they built
        From what they pillaged from your homes
To hang from them the gates they fashioned
        From your children's bones.

The barbarians aren't at the gates.
        They threw up gates
             To other gates
To herd us to the temples spired with gold,
        Wherein we're sacrificed and might appease
The gods they fear and thus ward off
        Barbarian disease.

The barbarians are not at the gates.
        Their loping gait's
             A measured gait;
Barbarian ways have been refined;
        Silk shirts replacing uncured yak pelt hats.
Yet farts still follow through, with orange shit
        Speckling their spats.

The barbarians aren't at the gates.
        They're far too great,
             And it's too late
To get all pious about integrity and truth
        Or simple kindness, with a rueful pang.
We've known them far too long so know that that's not
        How barbarians hang.

26 May 2020

When They Made a Scarecrow Pharaoh

When they made a scarecrow Pharaoh
    I no longer really cared,
Though the smile cut in his pumpkin head
    Was already turning mushy,
The straw stuffing his rich, bejewelled robes
    Was sodden with the damp it soaked up
        From the flooded throne room floor
And when they tried to move him
    Dead mice fell by the dozen from his golden cuffs.

And the seeds of rye that padded out
    His fat pharaonic arse
Became peppered with a bloom of ergot
    Which sent spoors into the granaries
        Borne by the gritty winds
Thereafter sending the whole Middle Kingdom mad.
But I found it hard to feel a thing beyond
    A begrudging sort of boredom.

That said, after the termites ate the
    Heka and Nekhakha
The courtiers bodged to give Pharaoh a backbone
    To prop his scarecrow corpse up
And he folded and collapsed
    In dust and compost,
I might have then half smiled.

For at that very instant
    a murder of crows flew in from roosts beyond the Sphinx
        and with a certain irony
built nests amidst the wreckage.

27 May 2020

Backbone

When you're asked to join the Cabinet
And think 'What jolly fun!'
And they then remove your backbone,
How exactly is this done?

Is it ripped out like Excalibur
Or is your hour of bliss
Disturbed as they dissolve it
With an antiseptic hiss?

Or, when you swap your vertebrae
For a thing you might adore,
Do they ratchet from your arsehole
To the polished marble floor?

But whatever way they calculate
To confiscate your spine
Do you think it's wholly dignified
To squeal, 'Oh! How divine!'

And if the blotting paper spine
You've now got's all you wish,
Please remember, your condition
Would disgust a jellyfish.

28 May 2020

Haircut

Ten weeks dodging contagion from a barber
Has left me with Victorian Bishop's hair
Until I sleek it back after the shower
And in the mirror a Victorian Liberal millowner
        Is now standing there.

You could pretend these chance tonsorial echoes
Mean something deeper about just right now
Either truths Utilitarian about Profits
Or more Faith in God's revealed Religion serves us better
        Than Science might allow.

39 Articles versus the Market:
Even boiled down to homeopathic particles
Both prick-tease with capricious inhumanity.
As of yesterday it's killed thirty-eight thousand (that's 974
        Extra deaths per Article).

28 May 2020

Pandemic Porn

Wanna Corona boner?
Check out a COO VID!
Thumb through our 'AHHHHH!' NUMBERS!
LOCK DOWNS! MASKS! FUR, LOW!
      Phwoar!
Cummings cummings cummings cummings CUMMINGS!!
      There ought to be a law!

What's that, mate?
Been stuck indoors too long?
You after something racier?
Look, come back here; we got the really hard stuff
      Galore!
Snuff movies, mate. A million of em. Gonna float your boat?
      There ought to be a law.

29 May 2020

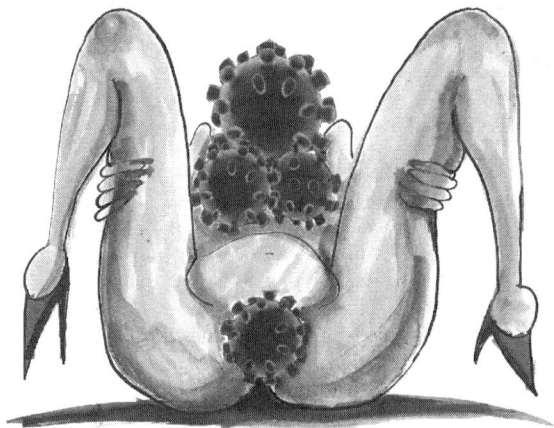

Spectator Blogs

Every time they reach
For the handgun of free speech
    Just pay attention to their other hand:
They're speed dialling the cops
To kick you in the chops,
    The cops that rich men have at their command

And every time they preach
On the godhead of free speech
    Pay close attention to their iron jaws
They don't want speech to upend
Their privilege to defend
    Their right to call you niggers, queers and whores.

And every time they teach
About the value of free speech
    Please watch the lips on either of their faces
For they'll fight & fight & fight
For their inalienable right
    To scream the shit that keeps us in our places.

30 May 2020

They Second Cummings

after W.B. Yeats

The Centre fell apart an age ago.
They poison falcons now,
Protecting grouse chicks
To be killed by corporate clients at weekends.
The loot is laundered through the flood planes
And the floodwater gets browner year by year.
They boast of their intense insensitivity.
Worse, there's no earthly chance there'll be convictions.

And the rough beast crèche is full to overflowing
With more arriving as each hour comes round
Til now there's hardly room enough
To slouch.

1 June 2020

It Cures What Ails Ya!

One should not mock the chronic sick,
And nor should we mock Dominic
Whose road-based therapies recall,
Damascus-bound, those of St Paul
Who was, you lot should be reminded,
On a road trip when unblinded.
Dom need make no apology!
It's not just ophthalmology
That sees Road Treatment's benefits!
It's a cure-all for the many! It's
A tested and well-tried procedure
From whooping cough to paraplegia!
For instance, the old dean of Keble's
Gout's returned: drive him to Peebles!
Abjure the lure of penicillin!
Simply drive to Inniskillin!
Infantile paralysis?
Why not try a drive to Diss?
Your child it born with a cleft palate;
Drive the brat to Shepton Mallet!
A cerebral catastrophe?
Fixed by a drive to Leigh-on-Sea.
You find your mum's airways restricted?
Motor her to the Peak District;
A femur pops out of its socket?
Drive all the way to Drumnadrochit;
Obviously, you have a stroke,
It's in the car to Basingstoke;
And likewise cardiac arrest
Demands a drive to Bristol West!
So if your stomach ulcer bleeds
Jump in the car and drive to Leeds;
Carries rot your yellow teeth,
They gleam before you've got to Neath;
Struck down with Huntingdon's Chorea?

IT CURES WHAT AILS YA!

Simply drive to Hazelmere.
A touch of cancer? With a whoosh
Drive off to Ashby-de-la-Zouche!
And when they say you've caught malaria –
Hull Regeneration Area!
Just even feeling sort of sick
You'll cure on drives to Walberswick
And when they say you've got Corona
A nice long drive to Barcelona
Should see you right! Whate'er you have
Just punch a route in your sat nav
And soon, on the A23,
You'll find the perfect remedy!
All you have to do is DRIVE! It
Cures what ails ya! Or go private.

2 June 2020

The Ogre's Mirror

An Ogre shuffled through his mountain throne room
And slumped beside the moraine of his hoard,
A few loose geegaws at the gradient's sill.
They landslide, hourly, to the cavern's floor.

This pile, his wealth, his loot, these spoils, he'd got
Bamboozling a dragon he then rode
On raids throughout the villages around.
He didn't need the dragon these days, though.

Despite razing their slums and silage dumps
The villagers now cheered him when he toured
Their villages (they're villagers; they're dumb)
To pick which of their children to devour.

The Ogre had cut off the dragon's head,
Scooped diamond eyes from sockets of gold plate,
Grabbed the rubies from its spilling blood
And, garnished with a child, ate up its meat.

The Ogre yawned, the dragon quite forgotten
(He stole some other dragons just last season;
The topsoil smells of smoke although it's sodden
With blood in villages where there's no cheering).

And now, amidst the scree of tumbling treasure
The Ogre spots a thing which gives him pause.
He held it between thumb and thick forefinger
And glowered. It impudently matched his gaze.

He turned it on its side in case its contents
Might spill out, then he sniffed it like a cat,
Was going to smash the thing in his impatience
When a tiny spark of Grace flashed in his head.

And thus he saw himself. He saw the monster.
He blinked. Then something else was there instead.
The mirror showed a saint with shaven tonsure
And a halo resting on his stubbly pate.

3 June 2020

Guard your Stash

Guard your stash
Guard your stash
Though your mouth's a toothless gash
Like the slits in all those throats which you have secretly had
                                                            slashed
Guard your stash

Guard your stash
Guard your stash
Though your ponytail's panache
Was, despite a certain brashness, thrown away with last year's
                                                            trash
Guard your stash

Guard your stash
Guard your stash
Though each time you take a lash
The pain and time it takes to do it leaves you unabashed
Guard your stash

Guard your stash
Guard your stash
Though you've lice in your eyelashes
And the rust will keep on eating its way through your
                                                weapons cache
Guard your stash

So guard your stash
Guard your stash
Because you still hold the lash
In a system which has spread just like a suppurating rash
Guard your stash

Guard your stash
Guard your stash
Because you gave the morons sashes
Which you can use as nooses and then watch the fools' limbs
thrash

Guard your stash

Guard your stash
Guard your stash
Because you create the clash
That your gunsels still will shill in streams of shriller
balderdash

Guard your stash

Guard your stash
Guard your stash
And then trim your moustache
And run again for office while you're laundering your cash
Guard your stash

Then guard your stash
Guard your stash
As your cops throw thunderflashes
Because any minute now this all will crash and turn to ashes
Guard your stash
Guard your stash
Guard your stash

4 June 2020

Tear It Down (it doesn't need rebuilding)

They tore down Number 25
Cromwell Road in Gloucester
But not before they'd disinterred
And laid to proper rest the victims
(Many of them his children)
Fred West had raped and murdered and then dug
      In to its foundations.

And now downstream in Bristol they've torn down and thrown
Edward Colston in the dock,
Boston Tea Partying the kind of killer
Whose trade gestated Those United States
Dealing in the blood and bones they ground
To line and waterproof the pits
      Of their self-satisfaction.

Let's list the things we should tear down,
An inventory of shame,
Those edifices pocked by Time
Which History pimps as shrine and not memorial;
Where the Crime Scene serves as sacred
To the criminals still sacrificing human offerings
At all these altars and these icons to propitiate
      Themselves.

Though when the bulldozers are done
With Windsor Castle, Bath, the Bank of England,
Oxbridge, Eton, Kew, the Stately Homes,
And blood bubbles in the rubble of the pebbledash
Of heritage & shackling charm beside the gift shops,
And that whole haul from conquest, theft & slavery
Starts stinking in the exhausted sunlight, then recall:
Swift, too, lived off the proceeds of the slave trade.
Because the thieves' and killers' projection of reality
Has even had its knee on satire's neck as well,
      It seems forever.

Though where 25 Cromwell Road
Once rumbled with the screams downstairs
        There's now a public right of way.

8 June 2020

Each night they tied a fresh balloon to
      A fence post in the field.
You could see them from the by-passed old coast road,
      A bouncing pinprick beyond the nettles
Each balloon the same dull colour as
      The last one, pukish ochre,
But each day with new words scrawled on its paunch.

The texts came clumped in phrases of three words
      In large and childish letters,
Illegible to the rare, far off and speeding traffic
      From across the scrub and cowpats,
Whereas the kine and sheep and creatures of the soil
      Clearly cannot read.
Daily, a fresh balloon's there nonetheless.

The harvest mice & corncrakes speculated
        This is an angel's lung,
Opaque inside from layers of caked mucus, a
        Mysterious gift of hope from God.
Some bank voles scoffed. A porcupine's insides,
        They swore. The earthworms laughed.
Although yellow the balloons smell faintly malty.

On windy days the balloons thrash in seizure;
        Flop limply when the sun shines;
Drum meaningless staccato freeform riffs
        During summer cloudbursts,
Deflating slowly through the long, dull afternoon
        Into shrivelled condoms
Pierced with petty uselessness and protection against nothing
        After dusk.

9 June 2020

Look on the Bright Side

Then we chorused to the virus
    As it stepped towards the door
'But at least you've changed the World!'
    And someone cheered.
All the virus did was eye us
    And as it spat upon the floor
What it had instead of lips curled
    And it sneered.

'But everything is different now!
    Nothing can be the same!
It's the time to change our ways!'
    Everyone cried.
The virus creased its many brows;
    Drawled: 'Didn't catch you names.
Though frankly I'm amazed
    You've not all died.'

We shuffled slightly nervously.
    With an embarrassed laugh
Someone said 'We baked some bread!'
    And then they coughed.
Hissed the virus: 'Heard of Malthus? He
    Could show you all a graph
To prove you're best off dead.
    Now just fuck off.'

'But virus!' we all cried at once,
    'At least you've made us pause
Our ecocide!' It roared loud
    'Christ! Stop whining!
You're just my scoff, you stupid cunts!'
    And left. Through our applause
Some of us thought, can shrouds
    Have silver linings?

10 June 2020

Sounds of the Seventies

Stumbling out of Lockdown
Like a 70s British porn star
Falling shackled from the wardrobe,
Streaky y-fronts round your ankles,
When her old man comes home early
       because the abattoir's closed down.

Opening up the schools
Like the janitor in 'Please Sir!',
Some kid's head's caught in the railings
And bodging up the carpentry
With make-do-and-mendy comedy
       and jokes about The War

Tackling systemic racism
Like a blacked-up back row chorus boy
In the Black and White Minstrel Show
As seen on prime time telly, and
Now headlining the Summer Show
       down the pier in endless rain.

Strategising everything,
A genius wearing tracksuit pants,
Dressing up like Jimmy Saville
In standard-issue rapist wear
And fixing it and fucking it
       all up with a sneer.

Crumbling a curly-wurly
Into his bowl of Special K,
Benny-Hilling 'Oo-er Missus!
It's getting really close in here!'
He slops in slugs of Rohypnol
       to forget the stench of death.

11 June 2020

Bad Magic

All human beings start out female,
The human species started black;
It takes some pretty fucked-up magic
        To turn all of that on its back.

All human beings are born as social
Beasts who need to help and share
But fucked-up wizardry has fucked us
        Convincing us we mustn't care.

All human beings are born to crave love
It's hardwired in as we gestate
How fucked up is the occult fuckedness
        Enchanting us to make us hate?

And if you don't believe in magic,
Are immune to legerdemain
How else have we become so fucked up
        We've fucked over the human brain?

What sleight-of-hand, classic distraction,
Ace of spades palmed up a sleeve
Could consequently fuck us so much
        That we believe what we believe?

That fucking chanted mantra: This is
The one way fucking things can be,
We're only human, & if you're quiet
        You might be human too. Fuck me!

This fucking curse is special magic,
Of church bells, banks, and cringing knaves,
Accountants, clowns and riot cops
        All underpinned by grateful slaves

An ancient curse that takes some shit,
And shapes it to some fucking thing
Waves a wand, knocks back a potion,
      Hocus pocus! Here's your king!

All human beings have been enchanted
The bad way, in this living hell,
So break the charms, spit out the potion,
      Crack mirrors - and let's fuck this spell.

12 June 2020

Playing Statues

Let's play statues!
Stand stock still,
Never moving!
What a thrill!

Never change
And never shift,
Just stand rock solid
Like God's gift.

Never give,
Never alter,
Never move
To lift the halter

Never apologise,
Never explain,
Never say
Never again

So let's play statues!
Don't move an inch!
All play statues!
    (Fetch a winch)

13 June 2020

The Con-script

A Conscript in the Culture Wars,
Press ganged by the press
To take the World King's shilling
And a mission to oppress.

Brutalised through basic training,
Then square bashing for hours,
Soon we'll be bashing Pakis,
But we're such a useless shower

Then it's guard a slaver's statue;
He's as British as warm beer
The serjeant-major tells us
And we're here because we're here

Then another camp to train us
To tweet death threats without fear
But we're hanging round for hours
Because we're because we're here

Next it's counting all the rounds
In the Spectator Magazine,
Then blancoing our braces,
Then it's chips in the canteen

Then it's off Psychops Training
To learn how to provoke
With thumbs poised on our keypads
The battalions of The Woke

And our officers exhort us
To go right over the top
To emulate the actions
Of a US riot cop

Driving back the SJWs,
The commies and the gays
Using earthy language
They won't let you say these days

Like in every war we drove them back!
The frogs! The beastly hun!
Let's drive back our next door neighbours!
Don the khaki! Grab your gun!

In their columns our brave officers
Screamed 'Better Dead Than Red!'
And that's the day we mutinied and
Shot our officers instead.

13 June 2020

Recalled to Life

You've been stuck indoors so long you're Monte Christo'd,
Scratched days runed on the walls,
Your eyes Ben Gunning madly,
So stir crazy now most mornings you can't stir.

You've been stuck inside so long you've gone full Withnail
Breakfast every morning
From last night's takeout's tinfoil
Cold Korma which you spoon in with a shoehorn

You've been stuck inside so long that you've Rasputined,
Charles Manson in the mirror,
Homer Simpsoned in your y-fronts
De-evolving til you're now the Missing Link

You've been stuck indoors so long you'll Dr Manette,
But you've been recalled to life!
The shops have opened! There's a fire sale
On strait-jackets and shrouds on down the High Street!

15 June 2020

Deathsitting

Every previous time they'd dropped Death round
They'd always phone to say if they'd been held up,
    By a contraflow near Calvary
        Or resurfacing for miles and miles
            Along the Road to Hell.

And even when they dropped Death round
To gather up my parents and my dearest, sweetest friends
    They'd get here 7 at the latest
        And Death would look round from DBeebies on the telly
          When the doorbell rang and sneer
            'It tolls for thee.'

But Death's been round here now for months
And every day I think I must ring The Authorities,
    And plead, there must be somewhere else
        For Death to stay, with someone closer, some family,
          Where Death might be,
            Well,
                Happier.

But dropped right in it, it's got to me.
Death's not easy. When we tried home schooling
      Death just drawled with unanswerable finality
            'Frankly, what's the point?' and sulked for hours
                  While I searched all day online
                        For fun activities
                              To do at home
                                    With scythes.

At least now we can get out
And meet Death's bffs off down the park
      Though if I'm honest, watching Death
            Morosely hanging out with War and Pestilence
                  Push Famine on the swings has palled
                        As quickly as attempts to build
                              Vast hecatombs and
                                    Mausoleums
                                          With Duplo.

And now the shops are open too,
Though I glimpsed the gathering darkness
      From the corners of my eyes
            As we queued up outside Primark for new cowls,
                  Though tomorrow I have promised Death
                        We're going to the Zoo. And yet
                              Amidst all those
                                    Endangered
                                          Species

There's just no knowing exactly what Death's going to do.

16 June 2020

Figures of Speech

When the stores ran out of similes
The poets queued all night
          In growing sullen anger round the block
Like a queue of poets queueing,
A line that no poet could write.
          But nobody was ready for the shock

When they then ran out of metaphors
And the poets, in a rage,
          Rioted in mayhem in the streets,
A riot of poets rioting.
But none would soil the page
          With trash like that. Such lines dishonour Keats.

Then the non-glut of litotes
Made them be not unafraid
          Oxymorons would be next! A living death!
A shortage of synecdoches
Would hancock their whole trade,
          And no periphrasis left to speck their breath.

But the shortage of superlatives
Made columnists and poets
          Unite, although its cause is no great mystery
For this means no 'Greatest Crisis',
Nor 'Most Fearful Time We'll Know'. It's
          Not even now 'Worst Government in History'.

17 June 2020

World Beating

(OR - BORIS JOHNSON'S WET DREAM)

I wanna be a world beater,
A world beater
A woad Botha
A veldt pouter
A white Buddha
And a world beater

And though I'm just a wet bleater
A warped boaster
A windy Bunter
My wild banter
Gonna make me a world beater
A world breeder
Whose whack butter
Soaks wank blotters
Gonna be a world beater
A fucking world beater
A world belter
Who would batter
The world, bladdered
And make the world bleed
Until the world's bitter
And the welts blister
Cos I'm a world beater
A world beater
A world beater
A world beater
Who's gonna beat that sorry world red, white black and blue.

18 June 2020

In the City of Veralynn

In Veralynn, freshly renamed
Capital City of Churchillia
Where the tannoys rasp all day and night
Alternating episodes of ITMA with
The World King's greatest jokes,
        The felon's corpse
Twists from the gibbet in the brittle breeze.

His crime:
Not mentioning The War.

Mothers turn their children's faces
From the scene,
Tug tetchily along the length
Of their fraying gasmask cases' straps
And hurry on to queue for hours
        For meagre rations
Of the most basic of Life's Simplest Essentials.

19 June 2020

The Great Escape

What if their inner spies had tipped the wink?
Foretold the cruel incompetence of
    The callous cranks in charge
And whispered the full consequence
    Of the old's expendability?

What if, beneath the cover of Lock Down's deepest anxiety
They'd made a Great Escape, furtive through the hunkered towns
    Evading the gerontocide patrols
To secret airfields under clouded moons
    To be hissed aboard the waiting, looming airships?

And what if they'd then floated, silent as the streets,
Into the jet streams to be scattered through the safer world?
And what if it took months before their loved ones ventured round,
Knocking on unanswered doors before breaking locks and lockdowns,
    Simply to find a propped up, plugged in phone
Installed with apps to simulate an isolated chat with calls
Made automatically in rotation, a trillion algorithmic permutations
    Of familiar inanities, looptaping on Zoom?

What if that vast flotilla then had landfalled,
Tattered near volcanoes, smacked down beside a wadi in the desert,
    Silhouetted deflating languidly at the jungle's edge
While its passengers danced with gauchos on the pampas,
Lured lizards to the pot through termite mounds
Or crooned gently with macaques sat in the boughs
    Of monstrous trees?

What if? What if? And what if some fifth columnists
Among the shackled vassals in Death's Realm
Had falsified the papers, sent their frailest charges
        Through the network of
The Secret Undertaking, trustworthy hearses,
Unapproachable morticians, unfilled pews,
Unwitnessed rites and unobservable cremations
        To safety and beyond? What if? What if?

And years to come, mysterious, coded postcards
All from the unlikeliest destinations, unsolicited
        And disturbing the still mourning
Are the only, vaguest hint of
        Something else.

22 June 2020

Yeah, Right

A poet told me Poetry's
                Exorcism,
A scalpel honed to autopsy the soul,
Spatchcock it on the slab,
Reassign your heart onto your sleeve
           The agony and gouts of blood collateral
                To catharsis.

Though I don't know.

I think, instead, that Poetry's
                Our birdsong,
Just the noise we make
To mark our place and twist our sweet survival
           Into beguiling the banal to believe in its
                Own beauty,
The way we once would rote injunctions into memory
           Through rhyme,
Tie up the tallies with alliterative twine
To keep them safe and close, mumbling
Metrically maintaining our best kinships
And coat the gaucheries of love
           In filigrees of glittering opacity.

You know, the same way that we decked
The dullest day to day
With gin traps, babies' bones and empty curses
           Back then when we invented
              Our religions.

Until, of course, the poet in us all
Was billyclubbed into the deepest dungeon of
                    Our bashfulness
With rolled up whips of written words
By grunting gunsels of the Priesthood of the Thieves,
The papyri's occult ranks of debts and death lists
Providing an initial, wish-thin papering for the cell walls,
Thickening exponentially,
          Built up with ledgers of accounts.

23 June 2020

Let's All Go Dunkirking

We beat the Hun, the Japanese
And now we've beaten a disease!
    VE – VJ – VV DAY! (V for Virus).
But before the second wave
Sweeps us all into the grave
    Don't forget a glorious moment to inspire us!

We didn't need the Yanks
Or brigades of Soviet tanks
    To define our mighty nation with their work.
The essence of True Brit
Is to roll ourselves in shit
    And pretend it's glory, just like at Dunkirk!

        So let's all go Dunkirking
        Because bugger all is working
            And the situation generally is dire
        And as everything gets murkier
        We chaps'll get Dunkirkier
            And victoriously sink into the mire!

It's because our Ruling Class
Can't tell its elbow from its arse,
    All these berks listed with peerages in Burke's,
Who drawl they've won because they've dared –
Ill-equipped and unprepared –
    To deny they've fucked things up, like at Dunkirk.

Posh, bland and mediocre,
Always in hock to their brokers,
    Complacent and inept, wrapped in their perks,
They'll still yowl of England's Glories
(Long since sold off by the Tories)
    With each fresh unfolding shitrain of Dunkirks!

So let's all go Dunkirking
Because the dying are just shirking
    Whether cannon fodder or some wheezing codgers!
If our victory seems quirky
That's because we're so Dunkirky!
    So let's drink all night to toast our ruling bodgers!

They'll claim the spitfire is their plane,
Churchill theirs, though Chamberlain
    Is more their mark (or Churchill versus Turks)
And they then expect our thanks
When they dump the other ranks
    At Gallipoli, and would have at Dunkirk

With their talent to appease
From dictators to disease
    Winging the lot, pretending it's hard work,
Unprepared and ill-equipped!
Then little people's little ships
    Save their bacon like they did once at Dunkirk.

So let's all go Dunkirking
As our wise rulers are jerking
    Around the BEF or NHS
And if you think you're feeling perkier
You are just feeling Dunkirkier!
    Dropped into one more god-almighty mess!

Because they'll lead you to your Death
With the lies upon their breath,
    Each balls-up blanked with an infectious smirk,
And this is just the latest highlight
Of our never-ending twilight
    That started falling on the beaches of Dunkirk!

So let's all go Dunkirking
Because bugger all is working
 And everything they touch will turn to crap
So if you're feeling irky
Forget it all and get Dunkirky
 And blow the whole damn bankroll on an app!

Let's all go Dunkirking
Although Nemesis is lurking!
 Sucking on a Duchy Original rusk
Hone your dirk until its dirkier
Slash your wrists to get Dunkirkier
 And dance across the beaches through the dusk

And we'll carry on Dunkirking
Until nothing more is working
 To be Dunkirky-wirky's such a lark
And then strap on that old merkin
And let's all going Dunkirking
 And reel all night Dunkirking! In the dark.

24 June 2020

Past the Pastoral

By now I reckon I'm way past the pastoral,
Beyond beguilement
Immunised against contagious charms

The shallowed streams of dappled glamour
Contrived to pogrom trout;
The hedgerows' anarchism, fecund mutuality
Shouldered like everything into the margins,
Edged out, then forced to fortress the
Multiple stab wounds of tilled fields;
The monotony of monocultures servicing monopolists
And comehithering the townies like a burnt out ladyboy.

And all of it as glitteringly contrived as an
18th Century automaton in subfusc,
Its china hands still jerking round
The same old endless card trick,
Watched with a soft-palating of gurgles
From the porch of Cotswolds cottages
The hue of earwax.

Though, for the briefest interlude,
As Earth tried once again to
Shrug us off like a
Lingering bad cold
The native chaos looked like fighting back
Before retreating once again to bide its time
And actually
The absence of that eternal trunkroad hum
Beneath uncrosshatched skies,
The patchwork silences below the birdsong,
Merely evoked an earlier nostalgic age
When cycle-clipped folklorists
Wrapped in tweed and tight ideals
Pedalled down the crunchy lanes
To lone, hagridden hamlets
To ameliorate Industrialised Warfare
        By confiscating culture.

25 June 2020

Fight Them on the Beaches

A toddler screeches
An achiever beseeches
A squalid statesman's backchat features
That fraying phrase from Churchill's speeches
The milling crowd, stir-crazy, breaches
Everything an expert preaches
While someone somewhere cites resistance

Lemmings are numbered with these creatures
A dropped ice lolly's flavour leaches
A fool who thinks he's wise thinks Nietzsche's
The cruel philosopher who teaches
We're all of us alone, and each is
Not required to give assistance

In midday sun a femur bleaches
A heliotroping sunshade pleaches
The traffic jam of cars now reaches
Beyond the Beechinged railway. Leeches
Must be factored in our co-existence

Skin burns to hues of bruising peaches
Highwaymen sweated in their breeches
Crabs seek shade. A whale beaches
Shades drift through shadows. Keep your distance

26 June 2020

Shame in Britain Day

Today it's Shame in Britain Day
And we've festooned the town in bones,
Coachloads full of local kiddies
Are off to conquer nearby towns
Enslaving everyone – for charity!
       And making sure that they record
            The whole thing on our phones

And today on Shame in Britain Day
We'll let the tyres burn
At the massacre re-enactment
Behind the Old Folk's Home
Before cancelling Best Kept Garden
       Because the best are all owned privately
            And are permanently closed.

Then later on Shame in Britain Day,
We'll chase away a frown
When we all loot the corner shop
Daub racist slogans on its awnings
Tweet death threats to our neighbours
       And pelt some passing foreigners
            With pocketfuls of stones

Then someone once off Crossroads
Leads the Big Blackface Parade
The WI's Cooking With Ketamin
In the boarded-up arcades
And we'll vandalise the floral clock
       Before they start the dog fights
            As the closing highlight of the day

And later on this evening
Inside the no-go zones
We'll be holding a street party
Feeding babies methadone
Then get drunk and stab the vicar
       Once his dad dancing, we all agree,
          Starts lowering the tone.

And if anyone's left standing
We'll raise of a glass of soapy beer
To propose a vote of thanks
To the pushy local worthies
Who've packed the Shame Committee
         And will fuck the whole thing up again
                 Just like they do each year

But not before they've stolen
The sponsorship money raised
From tattooing their own faces
By the local Girls Brigade
And fly-tipping on the promenade
         And the Sea Cadets firebombing
                 The migrants' hostel especially
                         For Shame in Britain Day.

29 June 2020

The New Museum of Shit

Once Central Government's Writ no longer ran
        Those who came instead agreed, before they shifted
Out of town to make up fresh arrangements
        To cordon off the crime scene, Pompeii that evil place,
Piranesi Westminster and let Whitehall rewild
        So that from the shell of Parliament and the deconsecrated
                                    Abbey
To the charred and roofless palace's facade
        Back down beyond the park and through to Horseguards,
All was now Chernobyled, out of bounds.

The radiation was just isotopes of long historic wrongs.
        Still, the mortmain of institutionalised atrocities
Wrought by the British State upon the world
        Made that bland acreage a no-man's-land
A haunted patchwork of disgust and honed dishonour
        Its gnomen this notorious coffinish backdrop,
History's proscenium arch, Shame's stage, Ambition's boards,
        10 Downing Street, which, however, they reopened
Some years later as the New Museum of Shit.

Satire played no part in its new function.
        The Museum's trustees explained to all who cared
That when the state collapsed new hidden treasures
        Had been discovered, sequestered far below the streets
In the medieval cellars of old Whitehall Palace, among old thrones
        And secret treaties, a stomach-churning trove,
Vaults filled with dried and varnished turds, a faecal archive
        Of the shit of all the servants of the State
Back to the Conquest, the spoor of Britain's coprocratic lords.

History can never be concluded;
        The heritage builds up like falling ash;
We need museums to wrangle our responses
        When the Past, like herpes, breaks back through our skin.
To which end, now with sensitive curation,
        The Shit Museum's collection was displayed
In recreated Georgian glass-topped Cabinets
        With rank on countless rank of medieval
Shrivelled twiglets shat by nameless clerks.

Further on, flaking Reformation Mars bars
        Were labelled as authentically the shit
Of Thomas Cromwell or Archbishop Cranmer
        With shining cowpats from Restoration Admirals
Filling up the rooms of most of the third floor,
        Then, after Pitt, more and more examples
Were kept in pickling jars, shelf after shelf,
        Pale prunes from statesmen and superintendents,
With one whole shelf of shit from Bonar Law.

A room was dedicated to the Great Turds:
        Churchill and Victoria's crap inlaid in gold;
Another to shit from unworthy recipients
        Of offices or honours, who had added
To the archive, having signed eternal silence
        In drops of their own blood as they had strained:
Kim Philby, Oswald Mosley, Robert Maxwell,
        From the shit of diplomats, spies and MPs
Right next to Sir Jimmy Savile OBE's.

This priceless educational resource –
        In terms of the DNA the shit yielded alone –
Nonetheless remained largely unknown.
        They gave up thoughts of opening a tearoom
As the volunteers who staffed the Museum retched
        And no one bought a single baked shit keyring,
Or a postcard for its kitschness. In the wilderness outside
        Eventually the beavers built a dam
Between the Cenotaph & where they'd killed King Charles
To form a dappled lake fed from the nearby breached Embankment.

30 June 2020

The Tower of Babel

'Look, everyone, we're in deep trouble,
Everything's a frightful jumble,
But we can come through! Let's enable
Our land to show them all how nimble
We can be! And let's think Global
And Build Ourselves a Tower of Babel
        Like that bugger in the Bible,
        An edifice to house a Sybil,
        A thing out of a fucking fable,
            Something we'll all adore!

'And look, I know it seems a shambles
And we, too, grieve for Auntie Mabel
But let us now create a symbol,
(Look, this is me being humble)
A thing about which bards can scribble,
How We Built Our Tower of Babel
        That rose above the burning stubble,
        A monument that we could cobble
        From the lumps of broken rubble
            Of the stuff we smashed before.

'This way society won't crumble!
And if you think it's all a gamble
To you I say, don't be so feeble!
Heed not the whining reds who quibble!
For ever higher we shall scramble
As We Build Our Tower of Babel
        Til we're hammering on Heaven's gables
        To face that oik born in a stable,
        And yank his beard and burst his bubble
            With a triumphant roar!

'So listen up, you feckless rabble!
You won't fit me inside a tumbril!
Our chaps have trousered all the roubles
To get you hobbled so that Dom'll
Lash your backs til you redouble
The Work to Build My Tower of Babel
        Then, dressed in robes of finest sable
        Stitched by girls with golden thimbles
        Through its portals I shall amble
        Before I slam the door.'

1 July 2020

In the Old Country Before the Plague

I

In the Old Country
        Before the Plague
There was that one day
Armand and I
Were let out early
In celebration
Of the President's Aunt's
        Birthday
And we mooched throughout
The cobbled alleyways
In efforts to avoid
        The Grand Parade
Til, from a doorway in the
Tinshack outhouse
Behind the Glass Cathedral
        A Deacon
Barely older than ourselves
Hissed and beckoned
        With a bag of gold.

The bag itself was bright chartreuse,
The gold in tiny, trinket coins
Dating from back before
        A previous Generalissimo
Debauched the currency and hastened
His demise debasing all our coinage
        With Magnesium.

Our task, the deacon whispered
Would be simple, also legal,
Though only silence guaranteed
        The bag of gold
And that was how we ended up
300 yards apart
At either end of the Glass Cathedral's
        Famous Crystal Nave,
The light screaming in like needles
Reflected from the buildings circling
The Piazza, their window panes and gilt
Cannoning back the autumn sunshine
Off the Radio Station, The Palace of Telephony,
The Ministry of Teeth and the spare, Modernist
Simplistic hulk of the newly built headquarters
        Of the Security Police,
Winner of the previous season's Architectural Prix d'Or
At a secret ceremony at a dishevelled coastal resort,
The award collected by a nameless man.

We stood, each wrapped in drying canvas,
On a little pile of books –
Bibles, books of diets, philanthropic reports,
With sacks over our heads,
Enjoined to scream blasphemous obscenities
To see if we could make
        The Archimandrite's niece
Up in the minstrel's gallery,
        Start giggling.

In this task we had good fortune.
Within seconds loud guffaws
Greeted our muffled imprecations
About God's Mother's cunt
And Christ's fat cock

Though the niece, much older than we'd guessed,
Still blushed as we shook hands and she
      Refastened her corset
And we ran off with the gold coins
Xylophoning in the pockets of our shorts
      The chartreuse bag an ad hoc, useless kite
      Trailing behind us like a simple younger cousin.

And we each of us now had enough
For three months of accordion lessons
And with what we had left over
We ate bowlful after bowlful of
      Moles jugged in wild mulberries,
      A famous speciality
Of the gypsy bistro tucked away behind
The Yiddish puppet theatre.

II

In the Old Country
Before the Plague
In the dusty gully
Through which the river roared
      In Winter,
Carolling songs that made the old men weep
But which now trickled like their tears,
Armand and I
Were pelting an old yak
With scraps of rusty shrapnel
Washed here from last summer's
      Air raids in the Spring.

But then, from on the gantry
Across the Rose Water Weir,
The superintendent saw us, shouted
            And Gave Chase,
His kepi flying off his head behind him
            Like a dove.
In my leather clogs I had soon
Made my escape, but Armand
Was quickly collared, swiped
And carried away kicking
To spend a penitential afternoon
Scrubbing off the crowshit
From the pedestal of
The President's favourite nephew's
            Tungsten statue.

Down at the shrunken river's edge
The old women scrubbed the icons
            In the purple water
Telling filthy jokes in high-pitched,
Pickled grunts, and cackling
            Like bankers.

III

In the Old Country
Before the Plague
After we'd been expelled from
            The Cadet Academy
Armand ran away to join the partisans
In their vicious insurrection, rising up
To smash the action of the
Ministry of Chthonic Culture's
            Cruel private militia

And I took up a boring post
Counting speckled air
      In the ventilators
Whining with a contemptuous disdain
Above ceaseless production lines
      In the burlap mills.

After finishing a late shift
I stood waiting for the last tram back
      Into town
Staring with feet-rocking ennui
Down the unlit street which
      Broke into gloomy flashes distending to the night.
Then I saw an old, one-legged man,
Leaning on a broken lampstand as a crutch,
Stomping along beside the ditch
      Towards the stop.

Once we were standing nose to nose
I didn't even feign eye-contact,
Looking out around his plumed hat
      For my tram.
Still, he wheezed into his thick white moustache
Ochred at its tips by cheap cheroots
With barking tales of when, back then
When he was still a Third Class General,
He led a stirring yet disastrous action,
The famous Last Charge of the Second Llama Corps,
      In some old war
Against those dog-headed men
Who lived across the mountain,
      Apparently Our Ancient Foes.

I glanced and smiled,
Relieved to hear
The tram perform
            A buzzsaw scream
Cornering an unseen bend.
He tapped his mottled nose and coughed
            Onto the dusty road
Offered me a pull from
The unlabelled bottle in his
Thin, three-fingered hand,
Its contents, limpid, puce, four-fifths gone
            Greasily glowing
As I drank.

Here's how! He croaked,
And vowed next year he was set on
Growing his own head
Back down beneath his shoulders,
Back to the good old days.
I saw that the approaching tram
            Was full.

IV

In the Old Country
Once the desert filled
            Suburban streets
And they razed the university
            To make room
For the plague pits
We were ushered onto the buses
And driven to the airfields.
Armand was now in exile,
Conspiring in foreign food queues,

After the Acetone Atrocity
At the Botanical Gardens
      Three years before
While my wife and children had been among
The very first succumbing to the Plague.

Camphorated tapestries hung in the
Stinking breeze
Beside the huts,
Hassled humanitarians
Gently obliging us
      To climb
The frail, flapping rope ladders to the ships,
Assuring us our bags,
Just meagre sacks with scraps of sacramental
      Memories
Would follow on.

A bearded engineer opined
With unconvincing logic about
New opportunities that would open to us
      In our refuge homes
As mad old crones,
Crook-backed, crooned as they
Cockroached up aboard,
      Insisting
We were being sent off
Way way beyond the Moon's right arm.

Soon, looking down, I watched
      As the steppe proceeded to dissolve.

2 July 2020

Hidden Hollywood

I

What Dorothy Gale would never know
As fitfully she dreamed of Oz
With whirlwinds all around her reaping Kansas
Was that her beloved Auntie Em,
Just 70 when Baum first wrote the book
Was, as these things sometimes turn out,
Emily Dickinson, bashful poet,
Whose soul would crack had Dorothy
Discovered even one half sprung line
Of Aunt Em's verse, now hidden round the barns.

She'd married late, to Uncle Henry,
Sprightly at 83 in 1900,
And in a previous life Henry Thoreau
Although he'd upped from Walden Pond
To make his own backyard in the Midwest
Eluding both the taxman and a warrant
Aimed against his type and issued by the feds.
In private, and out of Dorothy's earshot,
Last thing at night & turning out the lamp
He'd jokingly call Aunt Em 'Emerson'.

As for the Wizard and that talking scarecrow shit,
That was just their homegrown, to help the poor child sleep,
Augmenting the pharmacopoeia of opiates
These honest folk would purchase with dry goods
Across the counter in the store in town
Each Saturday, exactly like all of their neighbours,
In order that all strained pains of this rough corporeality
Be when occasioned eased towards transcendence.
Toto still slept on the floor, and knew Miss Gulch next door
Was being eaten by the syphilis bequeath her by her father
          Contracted on the trek Out West.

II

Whereas Bailey Park in Bedford Falls,
A handsome real estate development of tidy homes
In rivalry to the slums that Henry Potter rented out
In the carelessly evocative 'Potter's Field' estate,
Had originally been built on the site of a cemetery
In which Harry Bailey, son of the founder
Of the Bailey Brothers' Building and Loan,
Would have been buried had his brother George
        Not even have been born.
It is not recorded anywhere whether or not
They bothered to move the bodies buried in the cemetery
Before building Bailey Park, so rumours around town
That George was later troubled by haunting apparitions
Particularly when fighting drunk, should be reckoned
        Unsurprising.

2 July 2020

The Creative Industries

Then after that there came the sudden rage
For Pandemic Nostalgia,
The way you get to dampen down
The trauma from the stuff that happened next.

And in its wake the glut of Lockdown Movies,
A self-creating genre
Shot quickly, sating the demand
Of a shyly optimistic national mood

With comedies of family claustrophobia,
Sex farces where ingenus
Broke lockdown, bedding bored old broads
And melodramas featuring brave carers,

Their love interest a handsome young key worker
Who falls to the contagion
And nearly dies, but in the end
They defy social distancing and kiss,

Or else action adventures where a maverick
Government adviser
Thwarts plots to kill the lots of us
By cackling ministers in tall black hats.

These films helped mould the following generation
Watching weekend telly
When the current had the strength
Still stuck indoors, trapped by the murderous weather

Despite low production values and crap acting,
Bad scripts, poor locations,
These pictures grabbed the Zeitgeist's throat.
As for the extras, they simply dug them up.

7 July 2020

The Hard-faced Men Who Did Well out of the Pandemic

Here they come, the Hard-faced Men
Who did well out of the Pandemic!
          Buying shrouds to sell as facemasks
Pitching Apps to measure clapping
Sat on bodies doling dosh to
Other Hard-faced men so busy
Gulling ministers with bullshit
Filling forms on who to furlough
Shifting money further offshore
Scraping spunk from off the bedsheets
Of twelve million locked down wankers
To sell as protein supplement
To the clients in the care homes
          To increase the profit margins
When they moved into the sector
When things looked at their darkest
Bottom fell out of the market
With a mark-up on the caskets
Cornering the market
With a smell of burning rubber
Like the smell of crematoria
And you'll never buck the market
No you'll never buck the market
And here come the Hard-faced Men
Who did well out of the Pandemic!
Mark them well.

8 July 2020

The Hard Faced Men who did...

...WELL OUT OF THE PANDEMIC

The Things I Choose to Prophesy

It vexes like an itching eye: what's next,
What future is foretold in teacups' dregs?
But prophets simply second guess the scythe;
These are the things I choose to prophesy:

A second wave, harbingered by dark stars;
Boris Johnson loses all his hair;
Howls all night, as if nailed to a cross;
Matt Hancock's in a care home in a pool of his own piss.

All prophets simply second guess the scythe;
These are the things I choose to prophesy:

A third wave comes, and then a solar flare;
It fries the Internet, and yet before
Self-righteousness pours forth by telegram
At twelve dollars a word the mob gives up and all is calm.

All prophets simply second guess the scythe;
These are the things I choose to prophesy:

Zuckerberg's convicted in The Hague;
Putin, Xi and Trump, all in a cage;
Without the crooks and nuts The State's all done;
(After the Crass yet brief Dictatorship of Owen Jones).

All prophets simply second guess the scythe;
These are the things I choose to prophesy:

Fourth and fifth waves; unharvested crops;
Debts stay unpaid and soon the banks collapse;
Worldwide Debt Jubilees follow soon thereafter
With the new Crofting Economy and Universal Barter.

All prophets simply second guess the scythe;
These are the things I choose to prophesy:

Six, seventh, eighth, ninth, tenth, eleventh waves;
A Peace Conference with the Virus is convened;
Our reparation? We must now behave
And, as in Narnia, statues of good people come alive.

All prophets simply second guess the scythe;
These are the things I choose to prophesy:

The present locks our hopes in sequestration;
The future muffles all echo-location;
Yet still the past compels our souls to hanker
So push on blindly into Time: it's there for us to conquer.

All prophets simply second guess the scythe;
These are the things I choose to prophesy.
All prophets simply second guess the scythe;
These things can be woven in; they'll happen by and by.

9 July 2020

Hum

Frankly, this is none of your concern
And anyway, I quite resent the notion
    That this medium is just
    A doorway in a ghetto,
    Giving entrance to a cramped
Backstreet confessional.
But nonetheless, the fact that I'm adopted
Hums constantly, so constant
    That almost always
    I'm left blithely unaware.

But it's like Lemn Sissay says,
Upbraided by his circle for
    Obsessionally stalking
    Any mention of himself
    In any medium:
Without the third-hand evidence
    How's he meant to know
    He's even here?

Likewise, it's often happened
That I've glanced at a shop window
    Seen my own reflection
    And, for a nanosecond
    Wondered:
Who's that there?

It's no big deal, and anyway
I choose not to repine
    Straddling, like everyone,
    The chasm between joy
    And cataclysm
With the best part of the pleasure of it
    Acknowledging
    The fault's all mine.

Still, whether due to careless lust
Or being overwhelmed by this whole world
      Or browbeaten by
      Respectability and
      Pious eugenics dressed as
Good intentions, bathing babies by
The bucket load in great redemptive sploshes
Of embourgeoisement
      I think a thread attaches us somehow,
      A ghost-thin freemasonry
      Of once-upon-a-time
Abandonment.
And I speculated just last night
That maybe, like the dead or yet unborn
      At some Platonic level
      We all were once outside of Time
      Waiting to be wanted
In a place before the kindest people in the world
      Tied their new knots.

And there we lay, in cots, in rows, in
Halls beyond any perspective sense
      Me, two of my sisters,
      My friends Andy, Luke and Nick
      And further on
There's Aristotle, the Emperor Augustus,
Mandela, Moses, Eartha Kitt, and Jesus
Plus Edgar Allen Poe and millions more
      Just rank on rank on rank
      Beyond the Physical
Unconsciously anticipating an inspection
That might reboot our lives
      Which somehow welds each one of us to all.

Then, twelve cots down,
      Fuck me!
            It's Michael Gove!

10 July 2020

Cancel Culture

You'll be like a Roman Consul,
Like a strutting, lairy gunsel,
Fixed with aria-belting tonsils,
With lead put in your pencil,
A headwind in your mainsail,
Like a pirate on his fo'c'sle,
Feel like vassals storming castles,
You'll be pounding like a pestle,
It'll tie knots in your pretzel,
Your engine's gonna whistle,
Your dorsal is colossal,
You'll be bedecked in tinsel,
Music surges, like in Purcell,
Just feel your bulging muscles
As you bristle like a schnitzel,
Plus you'll drive like Nigel Mansell!
        Simply cancelling an Incel feels that good.

13 July 2020

Are You Ready for Brexit?

The combine throbs and idles at the crossroads
      The reapers climb down going house to house
From shop to pub they pick their ways through litter
      Til a trod on empty tinny makes one jump
Giggling embarrassed on the eerie pavement
      Bends to pick up his still jangling scythe

The leaves spurn sunlight on the crumbling wall
      Beyond the harvest, towards the manor house
Before which, on the lawn, the posh boys hunker
      Around the crate, to lure their hellhound out
They coo and pet and stroke the slavering monster
      With itchy stumps where once their hands had been.

13 July 2020

Mask of the Red Death

Now here's your task:
        Wear a mask.
It's no big ask:
        Just wear a mask
Knock some wood out of a cask
        Cut out the eyes
Then wear the mask!
Wear a mask
        Wear a mask
Calm down mate
        Yes, drain your flask
When you've finished
        You can bask
In our envy, but I'll ask
        Again
Just wear a mask!
Wear a mask!
        Wear a mask!
Wear a mask!
        Wear a mask!
No, you don't look like a Basque
        Or some cunt from Krasnoyarsk
Just wear a mask!
        Wear a mask!
Wear a mask!
        Wear a mask!
Now's the last time that I'll ask it!
        Wear...
Oh fuck it! Wear a casket.

14 July 2020

Banarnia!

Come on, chaps! Let's rename this land Banarnia!
Just one wardrobe away to that lamp post!
       What the snow hides is obscene
       In the Realm of the White Queen
That magic country ruled by dreams of ghosts

Push past those mothy costumes to Banarnia,
Frost glistens on the statues every night!
       Intellectual callisthenics
       Disguise our lords' eugenics
As they chomp Arbeit Mach Frei's Turkish Delight!

Just click your heels three times – you're in Banarnia!
Flying monkeys fill the skies, and no one's certain
       Which one of these is pervier:
       Bananas getting curvier
Or wizards fiddling behind the curtains

Mists roll away and there it is – Banarnia
So historic its past just keeps getting pastier!
       That weak sun is getting shinier
       As everyone gets whinier,
And moanier and bonier and nastier!

Crashlanding in Tibet? You'll find Banarnia!
That legendry land of eternal youth
       Where nobody grows old
       In our care homes, so I'm told
Our secret being, never tell the truth.

Climb that magic beanstalk to Banarnia!
Where giants stand on stooping midget's shoulders,
       The golden goose's eggs are guano,
       And we drink Americanos
While everything around us slowly moulders

Fall down the rabbit hole, next stop's Banarnia!
Once we were big, and now we're very small
      But because we once fought Hitler
      We can't see we're getting littler,
Cards and jokers tell us we're so tall

Jump through the looking glass – you're in Banarnia!
That crazy place where all is back to front!
      And you can make up your own truth
      Lynch the wimps demanding proof
Stirred by a farting walrus's each grunt!

The blue birds sing, there'll always be Banarnia!
Where we're sat on our big fat white bums
      Thinking we're Queen Titania!
      So fuck off, Michel Barnier!
Banarnia! Where Christmas never comes!

15 July 2020

Ghosts

All of us must wade through ghosts
As we navigate our lives
Thigh high through the thunderous breakers
Almost pulled under by the tides
Up to our knees fording the swamps
Over our boots in sucking marshes
Soaking our socks with freezing splashes
From milky puddles in the grass

The ghosts now trail behind like cobwebs,
Then bridal trains, frayed in our wakes,
These memories of vague acquaintance
Lovers, mothers, teachers, mates,
Who snag like ivy round your ankles
Or billow up in puffs of dust
And sting your eyes like pollen downpours
Then wind you with the endless loss

They're just our atmospheric pressure,
These ghosts of everyone we've known
And if you Muybridge any of us
Capture each instant on its own
Then restart Time, you'll millipede us
To weave endlessly through the mist,
Plaited with their ectoplasm,
Congalining with our ghosts.

Because, whichever way we grieve them
And euphemise they're lost or passed
The truth is we can never lose them
Because they'll haunt us to the last
Tugging each spare spur of memory
In our head's mad Brownian Motion
Scuffing at our hearts like emery
Tossed upon the ghostly ocean.

16 July 2020

Dancing with Death in Zurich

for Nyta, in loving memory

Yesterday, two years ago
When I kissed you goodbye
      You said
      'See you'
Then laughed and said, 'Oh, but I won't!'

You'd played us all, by then.
We'd done just what you wanted
      But I'd
      Not seen
Anyone who'd wanted something more.

I left to catch my flight,
My one regret: me leaving
      Before
      You did.
My fellow stooges went the final mile.

These days Death's date-raping
A trail through every dance hall.
      Back then
      You stood
And took Death's proffered boney hand,

You kicked away the wheel chair,
Shrugged away the M.S.
      And danced
      For joy
Held close, dancing cheek to cheekbone

Under the scorching mountains
Gavotting out of life
     You danced
     Away
Silhouetted by the lake

While we co-conspirators
Hugged the wall like schoolkids
     At the
     Disco
Too embarrassed and appalled to move.

And I still don't know if
It's the best or worst thing
     I've done
     Or both.
All that I know for sure is this:

Yesterday, two years ago,
I laughed too, and answered
     'Bon voyage!'
     Joking
Hallmarks should sell cards for just such things.

20 July 2020

The Besieged Citadel

In the last Act of the Civil War
When the citadel must surely fall
And the plague ran through its sentinels
The king declared war on The Moon
To prove he was a lunatic.
The sentries who jarred every midnight
With screeches from the battlements
That spies had made screeching illegal
And who then threw away their helmets,
Screeching helmets stole their freedom –
        The ones, that is, who didn't drop in droves
Beneath the arrows and ballista bolts
Hurled by the besiegers – therefore opened up
A Second Front throwing pebbles at The Moon
        While screeching at its sickled provocations

Beyond the dried-up moats and chewed dogs' bones
Of the citadel that must surely fall
Its besiegers glowered with envenoming suspicion
At their comrades, hunched to right and left along the trenches' length
Waiting to be triggered in an instant
To a fratricidal frenzy by a random misjudged glance.
Behind the lines another towering siege engine
Would topple now and then as weeping soldiers,
Affronted by some minutiae of hub design,
Would smash the axles in their fury.

Though it must surely fall, the citadel
Still vibrated underneath each footfall,
Its walls now mostly roots and fungus whistling in the wind,
The gates all long since bricked in, an Empire
As a last redoubt, a few enclosed and shitty acres
Of mossy, mouthy, mean mannered dementia.

And should any future Fortinbras
Be bothered to turn up to torch
The citadel, of course it never fell, and on
The battlefield they'd find
The combatants on both sides, mummified
By gentle breezes, slumping at their stations,
Arms filled up with bluebells growing through their tunics.

21 July 2020

Lines to My Dead Virologist Father

Now at last I feel that I can look your spirit in the eye
Now that at last the thing that poleaxed me back in January
Has been nailed down by a pin prick as the main event, the Plague,
That pig that left me sweating in freezing fits, embalmed in bed
In sulphurous miasmata, my joints like broken walnuts,
With hogtied eyeballs and less energy than dissipating smoke
Slowcooking me to Brexit Day, Pandemic's damp squib warm up act.

Now at last I know it's Covid, I can know that you'd be proud,
Proud in your quiet, unassailably determined way,
The way you were when I was eight and my endemic sore throat
Was, you proved, Coxsackievirus, by thrusting swabs between my tonsils
And drawing what seemed ponds of blood for growing cultures in your lab,
Also you'd be proud, I know, that I was in the avant garde,
Trend-setting and vanguarding the whole farce by getting iller
Than I had for fifty years or more, than when I'd had Coxsackie;
Fashionably early, struck down when our ministry of cranks was
Still too busy wanking about wrong types of isolation,
Back when the only vector was to be some foreign other
Back when they wouldn't test you til you're cradled in Death's radius.

Since when I've told the whole world how my virologist father
Would be laughing now sardonically at their hoarded folly.
So I know the pride you'd feel in your adopted boy's infection
Is bounced directly back, although you're now sixteen years dead.
And I repeat to all who'll listen how you told me in the 80s
When you'd overseen an autopsy on Britain's second AIDS death
That epidemiologically you thought AIDS was a dull disease
And that, getting down to basics, nothing that you couldn't catch
Standing fully clothed at a bus stop in broad daylight
Is all that much to worry you, if you take small precautions
But naturally, you added, the Establishment (the medical
As well as the political) assumed they'd smashed Infection
So the Isolation Hospitals sentinelling every town
Were closed, and as we spoke, now forty years ago, were bulldozed

To build neat estates of Barratt Homes, kindling Thatcherism,
Pump-priming the whole floating world of buy-to-let and outsourcing,
The neoliberal fantasy of privatising track and trace,
The brittle hollow edifice that's left us 60,000 dead,
Tsunamied by a dream of greed, a fresh Somme for the veterans,
As if they'd built their New Jerusalem on a burial ground,
An uncleared Native Burial Ground. Yes, just exactly that.
And now at last that I can look your spirit in the eye
I see it twinkling because now we know we bloody told them so.

22 July 2020

Fever Dream

I dreamed I saw Charles Moore last night
Alive in a bed sit
   But Charles, I said,
   That Kingsized bed,
However did it fit?
   However did it fit?

He said with a patrician drawl
This is no den of vice
   But Crisis looms.
   This tiny room's
My pompous sacrifice,
   My pompous sacrifice.

That dream is true, as lucid as
My dreams since I was small
   Which often fake
   Being awake.
Seems I've not slept at all,
   I've never slept at all

A weird and teeming world of things
That aren't and couldn't be
   While I'm asleep
   Furtively creep
Into my memory
   Of this world inside me

Jump-cutting logic my dreams serve
To scare stiff, or delight,
   Their clarity's
   Disparity
Entertains me in flight
   As I fly through the night

But when I had Covid-19
A fact that's now confirmed
      My dreaming mind
      Began to grind
As feverishly I squirmed
      And dullness inwards wormed.

The dream I had remained the same,
Repeated all night through:
      A rock, white, round
      Stuck to the ground
And a line I drew
      That was all I knew

I'd drawn the line with felt-tipped pen;
According to my brief
      It must be shown
      Beneath the stone.
Dreams weave their own belief
      But this brief brought me grief

To draw a line beneath a stone:
To get this job complete
      To get the line
      To undermine...
That's it: fade and repeat;
      Again, fade and repeat.

The line undrawn, the stone unmoved
No way to expedite
      This task some way;
      I press replay
Ten thousand times each night
      Ten thousand times each night

I don't care what this dream might mean
Or even whether it's
        Some shit that Freud
        Would best avoid
From my subconscious pits.
        Avoid analysis

And tell me why this virus might
In its murderous schemes
        Destroy the wonder
        Through which I blunder
Each night in my dreams,
        Even kill my dreams?

And tell me, in that Shadowland
We go to as we slumber
        And keep well hid
        Inside the Id
Are there dream dead without number?
        Our dreams no more to encumber?

Can we be locked down in our dreams
Can dumb disease go creeping
        To isolate
        Us from those great
Adventures we have sleeping
        Adventures when we're sleeping?

I'm lucky, because I woke up.
My Big Sleep? It's postponed.
        I live, to sleep
        To let things creep
Through dreams to get me honed,
        Things that God never owned.

23 July 2020

World Day Day

Today's it's World Day Day,
A special day to mark
Our Earth's diurnal round,
To honour the quotidien
Where everyone can celebrate
By getting Twenty-foury!
Make 24 new friends,
Plant 24 new trees,
Dream 24 fresh plans,
Earn 24 more scars
Although sadly, from Victoria
In Australia
Via Vienna to Valparaiso,
The celebrations, on the hour,
The kids' events, each minute,
And the son et lumieres at dawn and dusk
Have all had to be cancelled
Due to Covid
Plus, to be honest,
Complete worldwide indifference.

It's fared better though,
In honesty,
Than the International
Month of the Month,
Whose organising committee,
Made up of
Chronologists, astrologers and
Calendar printers from all the nations
Convening in Tblisi,
Once they'd voted down
The motion to rebrand it all
As a Memorial Month for Menstruation,
Proceeded to break up into factions,
The Thirtyites screaming imprecations

At their Thirty-Oner foes
Before a tiny splinter group of
Twenty-Eightist terrorists planted bombs
And slew their now all-male, blue-suited
Fellow delegates, and now, ironically,
After the storming of
The Palais de la Paix, are
Still languishing through more uncounted months
In a desert prison camp
While their respective Governments
Wrangle an agreement
On the charges to be laid.

Happily the United Nations' Year Year,
To honour the affrighted globe's
Annual orbit of our furious sun,
Swinging round in never ending circles
Like a sick and drugged-up wombat on a leash,
Has gone ahead as planned,
With some obvious curtailment
Due to Covid.

Frankly, the joy's drained out of it,
Even from the ferocity of adherents
To various faiths' alternative New Years
So when a family street party up in Bergen,
Though unlicenced, had sought
To join in the official fun
But just got tear-gassed by the cops instead
No one,
Not even the most bat-shit crazy libertarian
Cared less.
Indeed, hiding masked inside our homes
Almost all of us agreed
The earnest nerds
        Deserved it.

24 July 2020

Bigger Bastilles

FREEDOM! For which we all must yearn!
        Although it seems we need to learn
What Freedom is, what Freedom means
        To separate us from machines.
Though life's a bitch, and getting bitchier
        As the richest rich get richier
Our politicians grow more feudal;
        Their cops, to bend our knees, more brutal;
Society gets more unequal -
        Even our shit's become more faecal! -
To fight against the Nanny State
        Demands that everyone relate
(Say columns by Fifth Columnists,
        Tossed off by their aching wrists)
To FREEDOM - do just as you please,
        Be a racist, spread disease,
Defeat The Woke, catch the Zeitgeist,
        Divert attention from the heist,
Defy the lockdown, go to raves,
        While cops protect you from your slaves,
And scream and whine and howl and blow
        Your lord to save the status quo,
To smash the state but save the realm,
        While lashing fascists to its helm,
Go rohypnoling on the pull,
        Be free to keep the prisons full,
Freedom not to tax the banks,
        Or disinvest from building tanks,
Mock all thoughts of a better way
        And just secure the getaway,

And free to order in the bailiff –
     Oh, Freedom's struggle aught availeth!
Drink Freedom til you get cirrhosis!
     Because Freedom's Apotheosis –
It's just like in Fidelio,
     Like shooting capercaillie! Oh,
THE FIGHT FOR FREEDOM'S GREATEST TASK
     IS NOT HAVING TO WEAR A MASK!

Some say this makes me look suspicious,
But couldn't they be more... ambitious
In their Liberation Struggle?
Because I think they'll find the rug'll
Be pulled while they're clicking their heels
When others storm bigger Bastilles.

28 July 2020

Cabinet Haikus

Boris Johnson, oh
Christ All-bollocking-mighty,
Here's Boris Johnson.

Rishi Sunak's head
Is too big for his body.
Teeth outgrew his mouth.

Dominic Raab's face
Mirrors his charisma like
A bruised soft palate.

Michael Gove squats and
Makes the other gargoyles puke
More than rainwater.

Priti Patel? What
The actual fuck is this
Mad moron up to?

Williamson! He's
Wiry! A shopping trolley
On three wobbly wheels.

Grant Shapps smiles, then he
Looks puzzled, then he's solemn.
Boy with three faces.

Robert Jenrick sports
A phantom bounder's moustache
Above Bunter lips.

Jacob Rees-Mogg. God!
Spats strapped round an umbrella,
Monocle each eye.

Dominic Cummings'
Rapist's track suit pants. Fixed sneer.
A nation winces.

Who are the rest? Who
Cares? Spare my soul from stains of
Mediocrity.

29 July 2020

Hades is in Hammersmith

Hades is in Hammersmith,
The River Styx running beneath the Goldhawk Road
Having meandered there far far below the Westway
In echoing caverns underneath the Broadway,
Down deep where the tube lines should have gone.

Like Orpheus, I've stepped with care along the surface,
Gingerly from clinker traffic islands to the
Vulcanite pavements squeezed tightly down
The Fulham Palace Road
But far more frequently.

Time gets twisted around the edge of black holes,
So each stomach-in-my-mouth walk made towards
Charing Cross Hospital's concrete gateways
All happen now at once, although
They spread like funeral batter over two decades.

And then, apart from Russell
Who'd magi'd there to die on Christmas Day,
In due course they're all transported
Now divided between high and lower routes,
Below Charon punting upstream in a hi-vis vest.

Jon, twenty years ago, taken to the hospice
By the tennis courts behind the park;
Mary-Lou, fifteen years on,
Back home, around the corner, past the pub;
And now the other Jon, who came home shortly to eurydice.

All taken to that rough rightangled triangle between
Stamford Brook Common, Ravenscourt Park Station
And by the co-op halfway up the Askew Road,
Where people that I love all go to die:
Hades here in Hammersmith.

And just by its loose hypotenuse,
Abutting where the first Jon died, once stood
The hospital where I was born, and long since
Dilapidated into yuppy flats.
Abandon Hope All Ye Who Enter Here.

31 July 2020

Matt Hancock Haiku

Matt Hancock smells his
Soul corroding within him
Each waking second.

3 August 2020

Meal Deal

'Supersize me!
Supersize me!
Dupe a group to be downsized! Wheee!
Mea culpa wisely,
Hoop a prize, the
Thrill when ships of troops capsize! Flee
Snoops! Arise! Free
Cooped-up guys! Be
Cock-a-hoop you will demise, see?
Supersize me!
Supersize me!
Supersize me!
SUPERSIZE ME!'
      The trainee flinches
       Death cranes forward
        Drools from long, tan teeth,
         Sugar rush flashes yellow
          In the sockets where the
           Spiralling eyes should be
'SUPERSIZE ME!
SUPERSIZE ME!
SUPERSIZE ME!
SUPERSIZE ME!
      I'll have the Second Wave
      With extra flies.'

4 August 2020

False Dusk

In poor Beirut, spatchcocked and
 And fated on a faultline
  To the Omphalos,
    The keystone to the madness of so many crowds;
     Broken, seemingly, on concentric, counter-spinning wheels –
      Of God, sects, avarice, theft, revenge and power –
       And this time half-Hiroshima'd by cutting corners,
        Half-arsed 'this'll dos',
          The next last step to
           Who cares less, itself a weary stumble
             Before let's not even bother breathing,
I once saw, nonetheless, three different metaphors
Of Towering Hope in tiny, random things.

For if you walked, like I did,
 Along the Corniche in September,
  Around lunchtime, walking westward,
    To your right, beyond the railing, between Corniche
     And the steaming sea, on the jagged rusty rocks
       Sat burqua'd loreleis, knees mermaiding on thin, bright towels,
        Picnicking as their thin-limbed laughing children
Leaped screaming, splayed like lemurs, to evade the spikes of vulcanite
And splashed into the sea.

Meanwhile, to your left, once you
 Looked away from simple human love,
   The seafront's battlemented by vast apartment blocks
    Designed to block and then monopolise
     Beirutis' vista of that brindled sea still
      Stretching out to Sheba
       Which quinqueremes once crosshatched,
        Classically globalising
         Cedar, dates and sandalwood, the previous iteration
         Of the luxury goods, the Louis Vuitton tribute
Now encumbering the last elites, now
Penthoused in these Dubai watchtower stacks.

In consequence, a walk along the Corniche
 Got turned into slow motion strobing, a lethargic
   Kind of crowd control to bring on nausea and disorientation
    As the flats eclipsed the humid sun
     And every twenty steps, for twenty more you
      Passed from dazzling glare to moneyed twilight, and
       Shuddered slightly at the sudden cold.
Except, of course, that this is a
False Dusk.

The bullet holes still peppering the Lido's changing rooms,
  The wreckage, as I write, still smoking
   From the docks, the Stalingrad they wrought
    On the urban battlefield along the Green Line, (by then
     Rebuilt as high end retail to lure in rich thugs
      From The Gulf), the hatreds of Millennia
       Hosed with geopolitics and petrodollars,
        The Playground of the Med poleaxed
         Into an amphitheatre for unquenchable confessional
       Hegemonies, each ratchet down,
            The turn of every screw,
             Every floating final straw,

Nonetheless, is still really
  A False Dusk.
    The pavement's
      Glowing up ahead,
        Even though you clearly see
          The Stygian shadows stretch again
            Shortly beyond,
              Before the False Dusk
Fades away once more to
Laughing sunshine.

And six months after I'd escaped
  The Corniche's False Dusks,
    On my next trip I saw perhaps
      The most purely joyous thing I've ever seen.
        In the hipster bar off Hamra on the westward
          Drag to Hezbollah's desmesne, run by
            By the Commie Saudi, I watched young Arab
              Comic book creators dance,
                Swaying their arms that Arab way,
                  Like golden fronds of seaweed floating up
                    From some Phoenician shipwreck; dance
                      To other Arab comics artists performing
The Clash's *Rock The Casbah*
In Arabic. My heart still sings with joy.

And while the dusks, in all their darkness, won't ever stop falling
Dawns, you'll find, have kept on coming up.

5 August 2020

Beavers on The River Otter

The beavers on The Otter got all antsy
That there weren't otters beavering away,
Just gulls getting badgered,
And badgers getting gulled,
Dogs hounded, and I heard some hounds were dogged.

Apes monkeyed about; the monkeys aped them,
But then got foxed into ferreting around,
For a thing squirrelled away,
When they'd piggily hogged out
Wolfing the lot, despite their weasel words.

Some groused of being goosed. What larks, they parroted,
Then took a gander craning at some shagging,
The chickens never quailing as
They crowed and ducked the cocks,
Swanning around and wondering who'd swallow.

They finally stopped sniping and then they carped no more.
What bugged them in the end made them clam up.
The reason they were crabby
Was they'd earwigged someone yakking
About beavers on The Otter getting antsy.

6 August 2020

Urban Renewal

after Luke Wright

Past the houses that used to be boozers,
Near the nurseries that were once khazis
And the wine bars transformed from urinals
And the banks become bistros, then past the
Isolation wards razed for homeowning
In estates built where once they fought typhoid,
Boiling rags to beat tuberculosis,
Beyond cinemas long since sans celluloid
Converted to warehouse-size boozers,
Warehouses done up as apartments,
Whole high streets bricked over as house fronts,
Retail parks bricking over escarpments,
Railway arches now filled with ceramicists ,
Post Offices turned into 'Spoonies
By canals lined by workshops, now studios,
Where the sun never shines where the moon was,
      They're going to build slums out of face masks
      Slums out of face masks
      Slums out of face masks
      They're going to build slums out of facemasks.

7 August 2020

At the Warhol

The Art Cathedral's now reopened
And us lax sinners are admitted, slowly,
To the shrine, to gawp in studied reverence
At massive icons, now familiar as fossils,
Every last shocking atom of warm splattered flesh
Long since replaced by cold, hard sedimentary rocks of awe.
Improving catechisms on the walls remind us
Why we genuflect, and they've even done a reliquary
        By the exit, full of Andy's Wigs.

Though, shuffling in our masks,
It also starts resembling
A bad Venetian Carnival,
Put on by a prosaic doge,
Slashing costs in Plague Time,
The kind of Saturnalia
No one ever yearned for
In high dreams as they queued up
Outside of Studio 54
        Buzzing in a blizzard.

Still, on the way there, Compostela-ing
Towards the station, I mentioned how,
Back in the 70s, it seemed for weeks,
The nation was convulsed with rage
About a show on ITV profiling Warhol;
Mrs Whitehouse and the McWhirter Twins
Armed to their crooked teeth with righteousness
Behind their barricades of bibles,
Battling for our souls to guard
Our morals from this Tide of Filth –
        What we had, when I was young,
        Instead of on-line lynch mobs
        Gibbeting each fresh affront
        To everyone's hairtrigger tears.

Rose sighed and with facetious genius said
'I wish that I could go back to the 70s,
The Time Before Lies.' I laughed.
'They lied then too,' I lied.

10 August 2020

The BBC's Fucked Me Around for More Than Forty Years

The BBC's fucked me around for more than forty years
Since, just left school hired as a clerk, I found these racketeers
Refused to pay holiday pay, contractually mine,
Saying 'Not standard practice', the double-dealing swine.
Then – this was in the 70s, so please let this bit pass
As indicative (though then, as now) of the corrosiveness of class –
When I got that ballsaching job, stuck in Data Control,
I'd said, 'I'm off to Cambridge', just to show I was no prole,
For this meant then (might still do now), although it's a class crime,
I'd be Director General in about two decades' time,
With in-between vacation jobs, then trained as a producer,
Then clamber up that greasy pole – that's how these pricks seduce ya.
Except! Because I'd made a scene, said 'You're in breach of contract!'
When I phoned them up the following year, to refresh the contact
And said, with bland assurance, 'Any summer jobs now going?'
I was answered almost instantly, 'There's no evidence showing
You've ever been employed before within the Corporation'.
It was 25 years later, and with some exasperation
A lefty hack explained the cause of this rebuff; insisted
That my 'trouble-making' meant that, aged 19, I'd been blacklisted.
Time moved on; I started drawing stupid pictures for the papers
Depicting politicians and their various vile capers,
The kind of chap I think you'll find, with charm and – hem – some flair
Can help out our broadcasters in the filling of dead air.
That Christmas tree embossed upon my Corporation file
Seemed to pose no problems when I'd find, once in a while,
A breathy young researcher would phone up and ask, 'You funny?
Can we book you for this evening for 10.30? There's no money'.
I did the politics shows, Radio 1, the Arts: a slow graph
Will show my stock rise higher; then I did a show on Hogarth
To mark his tercentenary, drew them Hogarth's Roundabout
In the Style of the Master! But then I found some bounder lout
Cut the drawing, my masterwork! I said, can you return...
They cut me short and said 'We own that now! You never learn'.

So in the end *I bought it back; paid those cunts back my fee,*
One of the ways that I've been fucked up by the BBC.
The other ways are legion, like my surname mispronounced
(It's not much, although better men than I am often flounce
Out of primetime interviews because of lesser slights);
Sighed over freelance contracts where my soul's bought with all rights
To be held in perpetuity, or they don't pay me at all,
While expecting our blind gratitude, awaiting their next call,
Or when I did a nice thing in that nice post-lunchtime slot
On Radio 4. I interviewed celebs & drew the lot,
But when I said 'Let's get George Osborne! He'll pose for a sitting!'
They said 'He'll never do it. Who you think you're shitting?
But tell you what. We'll pull some strings and get Farage instead!'
At which point I damn nearly walked, and hissed 'God strike me dead'.
(For the record, Osborne answered – and quite without profanity –
'Please draw me!' You can never plumb the depths of these twats' vanity.)
When they rebroadcast the series (although no one had told me)
I joked to my producer: Do I get another fee?
She forwarded her editor's response, which said that I
Must never get another penny for it ere I die.
These are, I know, small grumblings. You'd never guess I'm born!
But after 40 years of tiny fuck-yous, you get worn.
And don't forget, the BBC has spent nearly a century
Insisting to our nation certain truths are elementary:
We all love Sport – yes, all of it – and we all love the Queen;
That creation is best nurtured through a badly oiled machine;
That each great piece of drama simply has to have a cop;
That management's like cess pits – the shit floats to the top;
That Northerners are funny; that everyone loves cars;
That there's never any money (except for bargefuls for the stars);
That the BBC is riddled with lefties of all hues,
So subtle that the bastards have hidden all the clues;
That everyone needs telling, save for those who should be told;
That cowardice will guarantee your chance of getting old;
That a vast craven bureaucracy shows Britain at its best;
That now on Gardeners' Question Time, hell! Farage is the guest!
So if you weigh its pros and cons, recorded on your jotter,
Judge it for the times it banned the plays of Dennis Potter;

For the way it offers 'balance', although you'll be bereft
If you think that balance means you'll get fair hearings for The Left;
For the way this crew of Wykehamists thinks UKIP owns our hearts;
For the way each frightened DG jumps each time Lord Reith's ghost farts;
How it's shilled for the Establishment since the General Strike;
And how it often broadcasts utter trash that I don't like...

And yet, and yet... The BBC, in all its tattered shame,
When targetted by Tories to get kicked and take the blame,
When Murdoch and the *Daily Mail* so hate the BBC,
That's when I shout from rooftops 'The Dear Old Beeb is fine by me!'

11 August 2020

Have You Done the Covid Test?

Have you done the Covid Test
                    The Covid Test
                    The Covid Test
Have you done the Covid Test
          I did one just last week

Had the shits and a fever too
                    100! Phew!
                    In bed! Who knew?
To be safe & be thoughtful too
          I ordered one online

I've had Covid but you don't know
                    Another throw
                    Could strike me low
So best to give a test a go
          It turned up the next day

Stuck a swab straight down my throat
                    Past my tongue's moat
                    Gagged like a goat
Then stuck it up my nose to coat
          The swab in mucal slime

We bagged it up – this wasn't easy
                    Feeling queasy
                    And slightly wheezy
My guts churning like the Zambesi
          And then posted it back

My Covid Test was negative!
                    I'd been a div!
                    But now I'd live!
For such a chance, what would they give,
          All those they never tested?

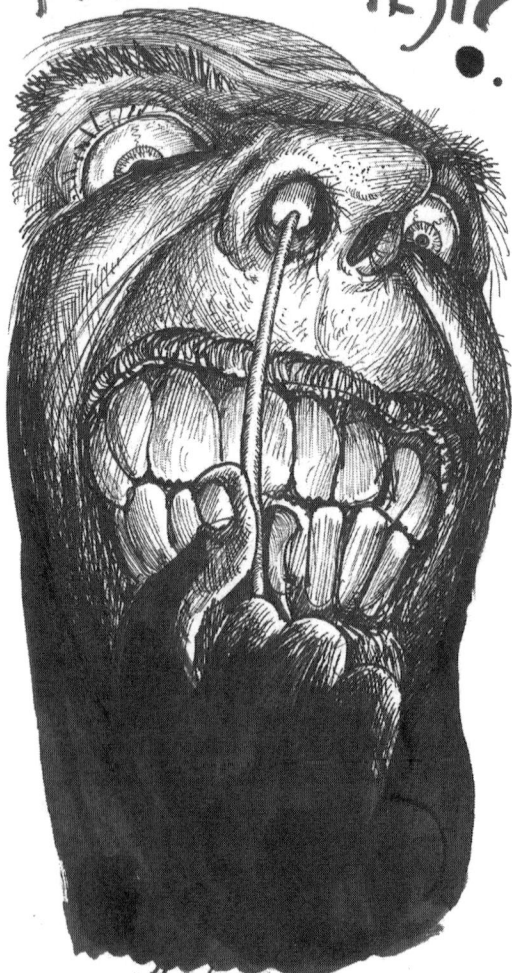

They never had a Covid Test
                    Were not blessed
                    Were second-guessed
And so were sent unto their rest
          Returned to their care homes

By liars, cranks, cowards and thieves
                    A family grieves
                    A mourner leaves
Death ever gathers in the sheaves
          Just never forget.

12 August 2020

Ricochet

for Jon, in loving memory

I performed my private obsequies
        last night with Scotch and white wine
Then bawled my eyes out in the garden
        as the weather finally broke
And when I'd visited at lunchtime
        We gave him days instead of hours
But he rushed ahead and died just
        after teatime.

Everyone has always measured out
        their lives in eating
And since his diagnosis we planned
        dining, once a month,
While time allowed, though Death's Pandemic spree
        put paid to that.
Jon was just a sideshow to the Grand Covid Parade,
        a small pernicious instant
Of what, we agreed yesterday,
        is always, always coming.
        Always will.

It's still cracked the World to pieces,
        the shards whining back to ricochet
Through decades,
        then forever.

14 August 2020

Dom's Got Rhythm

with apologies to George & Ira Gershwin

Algorithm! Got all data! I got my plan
Who could ask for anything more?
Got my weirdoes! Got my misfits! Algorithms!
Who could ask for anything more?

Weirdo misfits, Oxbridge wankers,
Foresee the future, paid for by bankers!
Lefty teachers, all left sulkin'!
We're just like gods, Zeus and Vulcan!

Algorithm! We're not fooling! We got our plan,
Who could ask for anything more?
Whack the unions! Whack the pupils! Algorithm!
Who could ask for anything more?

Whining children! Who they fooling?
Don't they see they don't need schooling?
Our new dystopia kinda frightens
We don't care cos we're like titans!

Algorithm! Got all data! I got my plan,
Who could ask for anything more?
Who could ask for anything more?

17 August 2020

The Washed-up God

It was, they say, three hundred years ago
   That the god first washed ashore,
Vast, indescribable and awful
   In every way you could conceive
And dead, long dead, they'd then agreed,
   But wrapped up in a cawl of death
So wholly freed from hints of life it
   Transcended comprehension,
Proving it as the source of Life Itself.

Its flat thousand-eyed face
   Was its first part to rot
As hunks of morbid lip
   Fell from its many mouths,
Serrated fangs dropped out with sighs
   And cells exploded in its brain
With startling thuds, and stenches
   That made cows gag twenty miles
Inshore blighted the whole land.

But as its carcass was so large
   The head – around a stable's size –
Was all to rot. The rest maintained
   A kind of stinking stasis
Which merely served to reinforce
   The thing's monstrous divinity,
Its leviathan girth, limp tentacles
   That shifted with the lice,
Tail flukes as vast as icebergs.

After several centuries even most of the pilgrims
            Breathing in gasps through masks of sackcloth
Furtively dreamed a high Spring tide
            Would wash the god far out to sea.
And yet its bulk defied the tides,
            Miraculous sour skin long since fused tight
To the shingle, while now rare borborgym
            Echoed in its empty bowels
Prophesying who knows what.

Occasionally a scale would float away
            To clatter like a hubcap through
The pathways of the empty shrine
            Where, only on the holiest days,
Masked priests would shuffle mumbling prayers
            Not even they now understood.
Up in the Castle the Grand Inquisitor
            Continues sending out the snatch squads
To deliver up more unbelievers.

18 August 2020

The Higher Theology

When you've sacrificed
      The Old Ones
And you've sacrificed
      The Young
To the blankly staring idol
      That you formed
From ash and dung;

When you've sacrificed
      Your servants
And you've sacrificed
      Your slaves
And you've sacrificed
      Your ancestors
By digging up their graves;

When you've sacrificed
      The shamans
And you've sacrificed
      The witches
And offered up their
      Powdered bones
In sacramental niches;

When you've sacrificed
      Your livestock
And you've sacrificed
      Your crop
And sacrificed your parents
      With your scythe's
Redemptive lop

And sacrificed
          The animals
And sacrificed
          Your pets
And sacrificed the usurers
          Who held all
Of your debts,

And sacrificed
          Your honour
And sacrificed
          Your skill
For sacrifice, and
          Sacrificed
The terminally ill,

And you've sacrificed
          Your children
And you've sacrificed
          Your friends
Til the blood flows
          From the temple
Down to where the river bends

And you'll sacrifice
          The Nation
And you'll sacrifice
          The Earth
And sacrifice each
          Living Thing that's
Clinging to its girth

And you've sacrificed
              All supplicants
With sacrificial
              Rigour;
When you hear, below the
              Ziggurat,
Someone begin to snigger

As you raise your
              Onyx dagger
To sacrifice
              Some more
And then you skid, arse
              Over tit
In pools of puddled gore

And you flail in
              Sanguine Slapstick
And you're sliding
              In the blood
Offered up in
              Sacrifice
To the idol made of mud,

This blank-eyed, baked shit
              Dolly, spawn
Of hobgoblin
              And elf,
Then remember, you must
              Never, ever
Sacrifice yourself.

19 August 2020

From the Heart

O fat white fuck sat maskless in First Class on the train
With, judging by your conversation, football on the brain,
Glowering like a fat dog eating shit out of a drain,
Sat slumped behind your table like the growing, darkening stain
On a passed-out drunkard's trousers when they've shat themselves again,
I imagine that you fancy that you've gone against the grain,
And you burn your own umbrella when it's coming on to rain
To show that you're a rebel who's entitled to maintain
That you can do just what you want, but let me make it plain
O fat white fuck sat maskless in First Class on the train,
It's your attitude that's unmasked, your effortless disdain
For everyone except yourself, so I will now explain
That I hope that you catch Covid & die in screaming pain
So you will sit no more in pomp like fucking Charlemagne
And everybody else can cheer & break out the champagne
O fat white fuck sat maskless in First Class on the train.

20 August 2020

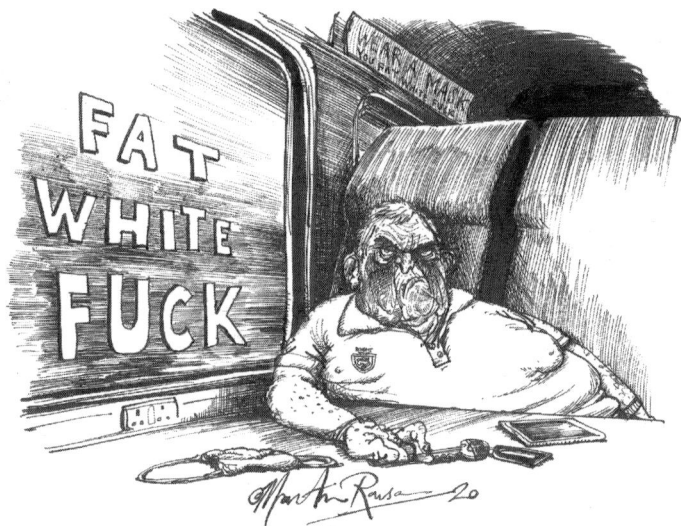

157

London haiku

London's Pompeii now,
Its denizens vulcanite,
Tube train catacombs.

23 August 2020

On the Way to the Funeral

The ice cracks like a gunshot,
     Cushioned in cartridge paper;
The forest fire crackles closer;
The encircling ring of rust,
     Eating jagged gashes in the
     Corrugated iron floor
     That jangles with forced intimacy
     High in the creaking scaffolding,
Tightens.

Death haunted my dreams last night,
With me explaining, in bizarre locales,
To long dead parents, or former friends
          Long since estranged,
How other people,
          also dead for Ages,
Remained so.

And yet, still half the world imagines
This is just a step to everlasting life,
An invitation to unending bliss,
The prospectus for a time share
          With eternity itself.
Though I continue thinking it could
          Do with improving its old sales pitch.
Right now, Death's still got a
          Fucking funny way of asking.

24 August 2020

Lines Seeking to Describe a Hangover after a Best Friend's Funeral

A drowsy numbness...
A lousy dumbness?
A blowsy glumness,
A frowning rumness,
A Fausty chumminess,
A ghastly crumminess;
A grisly numbness
A ghostly numbness.
A drowsy, Fausty, ghastly, grisly, lousy
Glumness,
But still we fuelled the flights of angels
That took you to your rest.
What, as they always say,
You would've wanted.

25 August 2020

Rewrites

Rue, Britannia!
Britannia, rue that knaves
Have for cent-u-aries
Kept us slaves!

Rue, Britannia,
You'll always kid yourself
That Pat-riot-ism
Will trump wealth!

Land of hopeless Tories, smothered by the sleaze,
Whose history is gory and riddled with disease,
Wilder yet & wilder howl the Tory Press,
Regilding the dung heap of this fucking mess,
Regilding the dung heap of this fucking mess!

26 August 2020

The Haunting

The second wave came right on time
36 hours after the curtains closed
With the kind of cliched crassness that these common rites
require.

And now Time, like a heel, contrives
To make the waves increase their frequency
To 24, then 12, then 6 hours between each stab of grief.

The sudden downturned mouth, the frown,
The sense of emptiness, the nagging fear
Of something torn inside my head I try to glimpse with wild eyes.

A pebble spat out of a pond
Might outfox physics in this fashion
And likewise make the ripples tighter the further out they spread

But that's the way all hauntings work:
Nothing to scare you, simply a sadness
Jaggedly soldered to the welcome pulse of any trace at all.

27 August 2020

The Hauntings

Jon haunts me in bright pulsing waves
        Like an early RKO Radio film ident;
Ann haunted me last night, in a cameo in a dream;
Nick, who drowned at his own hotel in Wales,
        Snuck in through a brief and callous text
        And haunted me for that whole week;
The other Jon, quite long ago, haunted me in the garden
        Unappeased by late night monologues and alcohol,
        And triggering an abject tic, as I'd look up
        Instinctively each time he crossed my mind,
        Towards an empty sky;
My father, weeks after he had died, caught my heart on
        Charing Cross Road, quite suddenly,
        Then sucked out blinked back tears
        On trains deep in the rush hour;
Then he and Jos, not even sensed but through their absence,
        Fouled half our summer holiday
        The week after we'd sold their home
        By leaving hints of all of Life's futility
        Lying randomly around my mind;
And my mother's trod my dreams for over fifty years.

All ghosts cling to their half-lives,
But however kindly, well-meaning or benign,
Just trying to cadge a light, a glance, your life force
        Or remembrance,
The ectoplasm still congeals as damp lint,
Slopping in to fill the voids where
Joy and hope have shrunk or melt away,
        To clog the soul.

And yet the weirdest shade to haunt me was myself,
When I got back my birth name (though no more)
And the ghost of Who-I-Might-Have-Been
      Sat in the car beside me
      And followed me morosely round, just on
The brink of palpable, all of that bizarre and long weekend.
Like all the rest, it would have been just cruel beyond
enduring
      To turn a single one of them away.

28 August 2020

Osteoartritis

after Shelley

I met a traveller from an antique shop
Who sold me a teak Georgian fire-surround
That, when I scratched it later with my car keys
Proved to be of plywood, stained in tea
And bought last week from Homebase, out of town.
This shows that bastard well our passions knows,
How gulled we are by snobbery & greed
We'll buy his pedestals and old commodes,
Even two vast and trunkless elephants:
'You've got osteoarthritis, your poor things:
Just buy my works, all righty? (then despair).'
Nothing beside remains. Round the decay
Of this colossal Wreck, boundless and bare
The lone and level shires stretch far away.

29 August 2020

Kinlochmoidart

Nineteen and I'd just past my test
So drove us all to John O'Groats,
My passengers now both old men.
        Both of them still friends.

With youthful recklessness I damn
Near killed us nineteen times before
Our Sunday lunch in John O'Groats
        Then I drove us South.

We stopped to pee in Sutherland
In a passing place. Clouds cleared.
First time I'd seen the Milky Way;
        Pissed over my shoes.

Then drove off through the bristling night.
Unknowingly, we aquaplaned
Fort William's yellow, spiky streets,
        An hour's drive from here.

By 26 I'd wisely said
'I think I love you.' You: 'Oh good!'
And with your friends you'd come back here
        Now with me in tow.

We sat in bed, gazed down the glen
On your birthday and sailed to Skye
While night skies never quite broke free
        From the May gloaming.

At 28, we're married now:
A mad fortnight of drunken nights,
Canasta and hilarity
        While lusty stags belled.

At 31, we're parents now.
Fred's 2nd birthday sees me bid
£10 to buy the show's prize cake,
    Making locals gasp.

Aged 38 we're here again
Before a damp cottage on Mull,
And their first flight. Diana died
    Later on that night.

41, this time my in-laws
Invite themselves, don't do a stroke.
We picnic on the Green Isle, Loch
    Shiel's burial ground

Before your erstwhile step-father
Drove us all mad half-planning his
Birthday barby on Kentra's sands
    In a howling gale.

At 50, with some fractious friends,
Long walks and late night whiskies and
At last we tour the Big House and
    Find the dog's gone blind.

And dinner in Acharacle
With Michael Brambell in whose arms
Guy the Gorilla died. We spoke
    Of foul-mouthed parrots.

And now I'm here at 61,
And Fred's turned 32 today
With us, wrapped up in Martha's love.
    Little else has changed.

Nino Stewart walks her dogs as
Buzzards shriek above the tops, lochs
Specked with isles with gangly trees
    From a Durer print.

In truth the greatest changes came
Between when I was almost here,
My shoes still damp from my own piss,
        And that trip with you:

At 19, on the cusp of hope,
Set fair for Cambridge, as they'd planned,
One life ahead of me on tracks
        Leading God knows where.

Then, whatever hope I'd had, that
Cambridge wasn't all I'd guessed, a
Timeless playpen of unchanging
        Old complacency

Rotted away to fuel that rage
That blew me, laughing, off the rails,
Spin in the air, then land wheels down
        On the open road.

That Post-war world of me, 19,
Was slashed & burnt. Yet thieves still rule;
The land round here's still lorded over
        By their landed kin.

The change is coming, like a curse
That festers through the centuries,
To pay us back in fearful kind
        For all our old crimes

The mists will boil, the bracken bleach,
The red deer drown as glens fill up,
The Highland archipelago
        Just beyond clear sight.

But until then, hope fills my heart
With deeper draughts than at 19.
We've all to play for, you & me,
        Still in our run up.

As the leaves are turning russet,
Cloudbursts pulsing down the hills
We measure out our lives in cats
        And trips to Kinlochmoidart.

5 September 2020

The Free Press

The trees rose in solidarity
                Refusing to be felled
But when news of this atrocity
                Reached those gold towers in which dwelled
The avaricious psychopaths,
                A small one of whose capers
Is to print lies about those they hate
                In their various papers
On sheets of extruded woodpulp
                They flew into a rage
And told the fascist lackeys that they hired
                To fill each page
With coruscating columns
                Denouncing those sick trees
And likening the wooden scum
                To traitors and disease
And calling on their readers
                To fight back! Take back control!
Chop down those commie trees and burn
                The bastards to charcoal!
Lay waste the whole damn planet!
                Purge it of each blade of grass
Guaranteeing that sweet freedom
                To talk out of your arse
Insisting all their prejudices
                Are Talking Truth To Power
When really it just helps pay for
                A taller golden tower.

But still the trees refused to budge
        Beyond some sacrifice
To fall to block printing works exit
        Routes, to be precise.
So the avaricious psychopaths
        Ordered their hireling hacks
To open a new front by writing
        Withering attacks
On every other type or kind of known
        Printed material
Which, the hacks lamented, could spread
        Diseases venereal
Sure to infect your kiddies, drive you mad
        Then kill you dead
'SO FOLKS!' they yowled, 'SEND ALL THOSE
        EVIL BOOKS TO US INSTEAD!'
They stripped bare every bookshelf,
        Pillaged every library
To acquire more printed matter,
        Through threats, blackmail and bribery,
And then pulped all written records
        Recording deed and name
To get out the next edition, headlined
        'MIGRANTS ARE TO BLAME!'

The trees just shrugged and shed their leaves
        Now turned a pleasing yellow.
'DEMOCRACY'S UNDER ATTACK!'
        The hacks and lackeys bellow.
But when they'd used up all the books
        (Not an infinite resource)
There was nothing left to print on,
        Which also meant, of course,
There wasn't even toilet paper
        For wiping off the shit
From the avaricious psycho's arseholes,
        Then publishing it.

They stuffed their mouths with bearer bonds
              And thousand dollar bills
And whined 'Writing was invented,
              As were ink and even quills,
So that avaricious psychopaths in
              Gold towers can tell lies
About the weak and powerless,
              And then praise to the skies
Our client politicians and print trash
              About 'D' listers
And columns by such massive wankers
              Their hands are pocked with blisters,
To help tease out our nation's Id,
              Promoting fascist trash
In order to spread hatred through
              The People, like a rash,
Dressed up in patriotic drag –
              Flag and Hope and Glory –
To furnish our gold towers
              With a further Golden Storey!
Attack any tiny part of that, and
              YOU'LL KILL FREE EXPRESSION!
(Though what you'll then freely express
              Remains at our discretion!)'

7 September 2020

Cartoon Animal

There's a smirking cartoon animal
From off of Kid's TV
      On a pastel coloured plaster on your chest
But if you wash too often
Its edges start to pucker
      And eventually it drifts off in the scum.

There's some scowling cartoon animals
On the ducal coat of arms
      Tattooed over the scab the plaster hid.
The scab is black and crusty
Like a dried hard dirty pan
      And you tease its corners with your fingernails.

And the scab's big as a grapefruit
And it softly tears away
        To expose a deep and ancient open wound
That's pustular and seeping
And goes down to the bone
        And you can barely look at it, but must.

Then you'll see the crosshatching of scars,
The tissue start to split
        And that's England, that is, hewn into your chest
By a millennium of conquest,
Dispossession, theft and lies,
        And festering with gangrene in your heart.

So best go to the biscuit tin
Where we keep the first aid
        With a Cotswold Cottage printed on the lid
And get an aspirin like a Smartie
And another pastel plaster
        With smirking cartoon animals from off of Kid's TV.

9 September 2020

Mantra

My friend Georgina Morley's
Mother was extremely posh
But had a useful mantra
For moments such as these.

So repeat it to bring good luck,
Whispered like a pacing nun:
'People are cunts', she'd say,
And that was that.

10 September 2020

Bystanders and Passersby

The obnubilating thunderhead
Of broken building, planes and faith
That billowed foully, pumicing
Those gruesome flecks of human bits
Down on the canyons of New York
Provides the perfect object lesson:
That the Chivalry of Modern War
Waged between rival dilettantes
Pumping up on certainty
      Is the bodycount of bystanders and passersby.

From stadia in Chile
To the suburbs of Baghdad,
Mining towns in Congo
To a cop car in Detroit,
Death camps, death squads, death cults,
In Ramadi or in Alabama,
Even to the killing fields
In care homes in Home Counties,
In war or peace or in between
This is how fragile fuckwits
Become Caesars, through the
      Bodycount of bystanders and passersby.

11 September 2020

No, I'm Not Michael Rosen

We're going on a bear hunt
We're gonna kill a big one
What beautiful day!
We're not scared
We know our Second Amendment Rights
We've got automatic weapons
We're gonna fire them from helicopters
We're dentists from Milwaukee
We're gonna get some trophies for the lobby
We hope we get to use the napalm
We hate those fucking bears

And those SJW Bears Lives Matter Snowflakes
Can go fuck themselves
Cos they're gonna go through the fucking roof!

Dakkadakkadakkadakkadakkadakkadakkadakkadakkadakka!!

14 September 2020

The Rule of Law

'Boris' has fucked The Rule of Law!
And what's in there not to adore?
Now we can batter down his door.
And piss upon his parquet floor,
Steal everything he's got, and more,
Then sock the fucker on the jaw
And he can't even call The Law!

And twats straight out of Evelyn Waugh
Survey vast tracts of fen and moor
Their family's owned since days of yore
And every fat complacent boor
Assumes they'll own it evermore –
But not without The Rule of Law!

For 'libertarians' ignore
That mutual aid's required before
You smash the state and ditch the law.
They think that they can simply whore
After loot and furthermore,
Unbound by rules that they deplore,
They can pillage even more
And stash the swag safely offshore!

But typically, they don't explore
The flipside in this tug-o-war:
That WE can steal from THEM, and nor
Can they stop us, without The Law.
Nor will the sound of dropping jaw
Of Tories who've been so cocksure
Prevent the spilling of their gore
Without protection of The Law.

So now they've dumped The Rule of Law
Let's prise open their grasping claw,
Deprive them of their homes galore,
Smash their Oxbridge boatclub oar,
Land our ships upon their shore,
Bring down our hammers just like Thor
As we even up the score.

And if they scream 'WHERE IS THE LAW?'
They should've thought of that before
They let 'Boris' fuck The Law.

15 September 2020

Definitions of the Rule of Six

That period of Tyranny
In the Khanate of The Golden Horde
When the infant khan's six uncles
Despoiled the land until each one
Was strangled by a Kurdish eunuch
Himself then sacrificed in gratitude
To their gods of
Steppe and eagle's cry.

That Pythagorean formula
That proves that six,
Divided by itself, is
Neither greater nor lesser
Than the sum of its own square root
Subdivided by itself.

The title of a Sherlock Holmes
Mystery somehow involving
Half a cricket team
That Conan Doyle himself
Burnt in the grate
Once he perceived
It was, after reflection, just
Too farfetched and ridiculous.

A lost bejewelled straight edge
For measuring the Golden Mean
Created by Fermat himself
To measure the immeasurable
Until Descartes, with a dirty laugh,
Claimed it was the length of Fermat's cock.
They say the rule was melted down
By order of a secret Papal Court.

The mocking epitaph scratched on
The cell doors which served as tombstones,
Of those now nameless functionaries
Who, the legends say, coined a phrase
Of such aching banality, not fiendishly
Thus to disguise the true despotic nature
Of their draconian edict
But just because they were themselves banal.
The words – it's claimed they are the same –
Were scratched by unknown hands
Some centuries after The Reckoning
By which time tempers
Had somewhat cooled.

16 September 2020

Arsing at the Wake

Like any decent person would
We stared unspeaking at our drinks
Still pretending not to hear them
      Arsing at the Wake

They say they're her rich relatives
Although we've never met before
Their teenager's now doing handstands
      Arsing at the Wake

The ashtray's full up on the coffin,
Their glasses stain rings on its lid
Some woman howls in raucous grief
      Arsing at the Wake

That man's now bragging on their closeness
And braying about all he did
To comfort her when she was dying
      Arsing at the Wake

Although we've heard they robbed her blind
Then made her go out on the game
And beat her til she gave her passwords
      Arsing at the Wake

They never phoned, they'd never visit,
They never sent a Christmas card,
But now they drawl how much they loved her
      Arsing at the Wake

That souvenir from Ghent's just smashed.
She promised that to us, you know.
Somehow the curtains have caught fire.
      Arsing at the Wake

Those boys've opened up the coffin.
They've sat her up and raised a glass
To pour more sherry through her stiff lips
      Arsing at the Wake

A drunken uncle's mawkishly
Slurring that she's still alive,
And that they'll both now go out clubbing
      Arsing at the Wake

They've emptied out the cabinets
And trodden quiche into the rug
And now they're tearing up her photos
      Arsing at the Wake

We've been locked in an upstairs closet.
Downstairs the hoots and screams get worse.
Smoke's seeping beneath the door now.
      Arsing at the Wake.

17 September 2020

Regressional

after Kipling

God of Our Fathers, down in Hell,
    God of Thunder, Trees and Drums,
There's still so much stuff left to sell,
    So many contracts for our chums –
Lord God of Lies, fill up our cup:
There's still so much left to fuck up!

Some crusties in a care home died;
    The weirdos and the misfits swarm;
A mediocre place man lied
    Because that kind of thing's the norm –
Lord God of Death, please let us sup!
There's still so much left to fuck up!

For thee we shrug off all disgrace,
    Responsibility all ducked,
And give thee, Lord, this Track & Trace
    That Dido Queen of Carnage fucked –
Lord God, we'll sacrifice a pup!
There's so much left still to fuck up!

And though our Prime Minister's crap
    And we fear his spermatozoa
Is past its peak, the poor old chap,
    Blown out just like Krakatoa –
Lord God of Spaff, please let him tup –
There's so much still left to fuck up.

Until we've fucked up everything,
    Destroyed the country, thieved it all,
Please heed this hymn to thee we sing
    In our complacent, languid drawl –
Grant us your blessing as reward:
We fucked it up for thee, O Lord!

17 September 2020

The UroBoris

The snake coils round again and starts devouring its own tail
   The scorpion arches up to lick its sting
The cassowary bends to peck at its own poisoned spur
   And in a yogic miracle Johnson kisses his own ring.

Covid swerves in a tight circle and starts over again
   Old No-Eyes frugs a circuit with his scythe
And Johnson fists himself with his own tousled turnip head
   Though none of us would ever guess the wanker was so lithe.

Everything comes round again, eternally recurring,
   In endless repetition, like a comet.
Johnson sticks his head up his loose arse biting at Brexit Deals
   Like a fat, thrashed dog returning every evening to its vomit.

18 September 2020

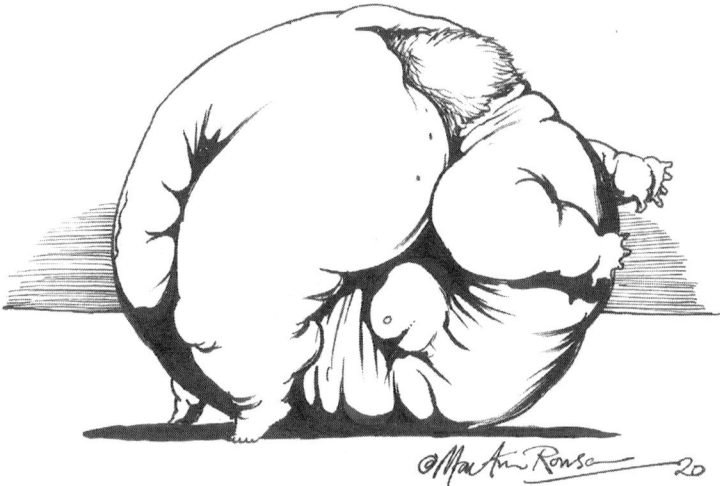

The Second Wave

after Stevie Smith

Not waving, but drowning;
Not saving, just frowning,
Misbehaving and downing
And raving, ungowning,
Enslaving, crackdowning,
And craving renown in
Waiving, letdowning;
Not braving, but browning;
Not slaving; just clowning.
Engraving breakdowning.
Microwaving.
Meltdowning.
Not waving.
But drowning.

20 September 2020

The Evening of Sunday 20 September 2020

You know that moment?
That moment – just an instant –
When you've had the slightly drunken row
With both the cooking and yourself
And for a brigadooning second you see the final truth?

And it's damp, old, splintering timber,
Dark brown and splaying at its hacked and broken ends,
Spanning an abyss which is itself
Black and deepening red?

And then the end of that unfinished bridge
Is all the fucking thing that you can't see?
Well, that, along, just beyond
The corner of your eye,
The crispy, tissue thin yet brittle
Edge of eternally recurring sadness
When the September nights turn on us again
And start closing in
Circumferencing everything.

That. Forever,
Before a second later
I blink and pull myself together
And let my heart, pro tem, fill back up
With joy. But can't you see?

21 September 2020

The Twin Pillars of Wisdom of Bill Atkins

Bill Atkins was a small-scale dealer
        Who specialised in making deals
Selling grass to public schoolboys;
        To be precise, to friends of mine.
I'll admit it: buying drugs,
        Like voting Tory, is not my game;
The protocols involved elude me,
        So I'd smoke other people's stash.
But that's the way I knew Bill Atkins:
        My mates dropped by his Northwood flat,
A ground floor bedsit, weirdly tidy,
        That smelled of amyl and stale spunk,
To score a bag of this or that,
        With me in tow, quietly observing.
I doubt he even noticed me,
        Another punter passing through,
But I noticed his large, square head,
        His haircut that didn't quite fit,
His rangey good spirits and the way he
        Spouted wisdom of a sort.

He's long dead now, a brief statistic,
        In a file that's since been lost,
Dying in custody, another
        Instance of the silent pogrom
It's indecent even mentioning,
        The ways they've always cleared up crime.
And even if, in those ecologies
        Where he fulfilled an obvious need,
I got a sense of barrel scraping
        Selling dope to twats like us,

In druggie terms, the rough equivalent
        Of cabbies on the Heathrow run,
Not quite as bad as pills for schoolkids
        But hardly Pablo Escobar,
But nonetheless he deserved better
        Than dying in an echoing cell
With a knee pressed on his neck
        As the filth put out the trash
Entrenched, beyond reach of redemption,
        Deep in The Disposable.

Yet, in his time, he spouted wisdom,
        Of his time, and of himself;
Foul, brutal wisdom, best forgotten,
        But still wisdom, nonetheless.
So, having acted out the courtesies
        And had a smoke to seal the deal
If you found you couldn't now drive
        'Have a drink!' Bill would espouse.
Likewise, if drunk, a spliff would sort you,
        And thus restore the Cosmic Balance,
Rebalancing the Humours,
        Propitiating his stoned Zen.
'All women like to be knocked around,'
        He'd then say with a crooked grin,
'And those who say they don't are lying!'
        We'd laugh at him, and he'd laugh back,
And no one sought to put him right
        Beyond a mockney slew of swearing,
For after all, what was the point?
        He was only selling grass.

And yet, beyond the grave, Bill Atkins
                Spreads a hand around the globe
Establishing new paradigms,
                Underpinned by jokes and violence,
That anyone who disagrees
                Isn't expressing an opinion,
But lying, lying in their teeth,
                To trap you in their evil plot.
Thus entrenched, your rectitude
                Is buttressed by the frightful fact
That your opponents are so evil
                They lie to douse your burning truth.
And No means Yes, and all is Fake News
                As part of vast conspiracies,
A comfort blanket for extinction
                A mindset for the Final Days
An insight from a dead drug dealer's
                Northwood bedsit, the crucible –
Aping Marx's British Library –
                For Our Last Enlightenment.

22 September 2020

Marvel Univers(al Truth)

A culture that needs
    Superheroes
Also needs an
    Underclass
Whose homegrown heroes are
    Supernumerary
To the requirements of the Supervillains
    Who are actually in charge.

23 September 2020

Friends

Are you maybe Friends with a Museum,
Or a Hospital? And how's that working out?
And is it for their bants, or for their pub jokes,
Or because they'll be there for you when you're down?
Or have you fatally miscalculated
The nature of this friendship after all?

That really you're just no more than a sidekick?
Part of an entourage to big them up
On the promise that one day, if you stay loyal,
They let you see one of their prized possessions
Or meet them, round the back, and secretly
See where they dump the bandages and stiffs?

All in all, with friends like this, I reckon
Your need to make some more friends your own age.

24 September 2020

And Lovers

Do you love your country? So, is it your lover?
Do you engage in foreplay? Tenderly?
Does it say 'I love you', then bring flowers,
Whispering sweet nothings in your ear?

Or does it simply offer tracts of soil?
Maybe a mountain top too, if you're good?
Then press your face against the cupboard wall
And push its thick, brash, sweaty bulk against you
Before withdrawing, sated, hum a tune
And drawl 'stop snivelling' as it kills the light?

Do you lick your bruised lip as its dinner's cooling
Kidding yourself that it'll be home soon,
When you know it's downtown with its cronies,
A geopolitical posse on the corner,
Flaunting paunches, jeering at the women
Until the whole gang flash their crinkled cocks,
Start fights and then see who can piss the highest
Up against the burnt-out nursery's wall?

And does your heart beat faster as the key turns
At midnight and you straighten what you wear
And wipe your face and smile with desperation
As your country thuds against stuff in the hall,
Stumbling as it unfastens its belt?
And anyway, so how did you two first meet?
You think you've known your lover all your life?
You say you think it might have always been here?
You think maybe your lover is... your parent?!
Sweet Jesus Christ! You ought to ring a helpline!

Phone the police! Or stab it in the eye!
Flee to a refuge!

But, then, refugees,
Having run away from their abusers
Now find themselves besieged by other lovers,
Patriaphiliacs who'll burn their camps down,
Country lovers fuelled by needy yearning
Whose love is cushioned in their hearts by hate,
Hate in their hearts that's fired as hard as granite.

Then does your country thumb away your teardrops,
Propose a singsong to get your pecker up
And brag about the cellars full of lovers,
Told to try and win their country's love,
Like those who proved their love & earned requiting,
Now at rest beneath the patio?

By all mean love your country if you must do,
If you like loving endless fields of mud
And the thieves and thugs who own and plough them,
Just don't imagine that it loves you back.
It's far too old and jaded to broach romance –
Admit you're just another one night stand.

24 September 2020

The Grand Gesture

When we're out the other side
   And no one's died for 30 days
We shall all convene to plan
   For The Grand Gesture.

We're going to boost the public mood
   And bring our country back as one.
We've all been through this thing and so
   We'll need A Grand Gesture.

Something to set our hearts alight.
   Something to make us smile again
Something that restores our pride:
   In short, A Grand Gesture.

And we're the people for this task,
   Well connected, well-to-do;
Good, Great, with get up and go.
   Let's plan The Grand Gesture.

Think it's our blithe complacency,
   Our easy charm, that does the trick.
Noticed it at Balliol
   Making grand gestures.

And so we'll ring up some old pals,
   Some bffs from tennis courts,
To pitch in for the tendering thing
   For The Grand Gesture

And then we'll sit for hours and hours
   Watching endless PowerPoints,
Donning wellies touring sites
   For The Grand Gesture

The Grand Gesture

And now at last the tendering
      Process will be done and dusted
So we'll called a Presser to
      Announce The Grand Gesture.

A thing that justifies itself
      And speaks to all in our great land.
The enterprise of its fair folk.
      This Beautiful Grand Gesture.

I'll say, You'll know these boys. They're great.
      I knew their CEO at Stowe.
They're just the chaps to do us proud
      Building The Grand Gesture.

And the winning entry is...
      We'll stoke the tension up a bit....
A NEW TITANIC!!
      Just the thing for The Grand Gesture.

Stylish, graceful, built to last,
      A sleek streak on the Ocean Waves
The Past and Future forged as One
      A Truly Grand Gesture.

The team's already hard at work.
      Their track record's second to none.
Building icebergs round the world.
      HURRAH FOR THE GRAND GESTURE.

25 September 2020

Inward Eye

That thing when, in repose,
        You get
A sudden softening, as if
        You're being folded
In choux pastry, the floating and caressing
        Comfort of
Sunday evening freshly laundered sheets

It's that, that jolt donated by
        A random
Recollection of passed bliss,
        Like this morning,
And the memory of dead Ginger
        Our blind dog,
Tethered to the seat beside me
        As I drove her home
From the Goose Green poodle parlour
        And she began
To howl and yelp, in time and in tune
        With me as I sang along
To Herb Alpert's 'This Guy's In Love'
        Playing on my iPod through the car.

And the facts, that she went deaf
        And then she died
And life is finite and endlessly
        Assaulted by
Both sadness and dismay,
        All that gets airbrushed out
Then hosed away from round the
        Spotlit pinpoint of pure joy
And the eternity of the moment.

Wordsworth, I guess, must have
        Felt like that,
Remembering those bloody flowers,
        Though Ginger,
Visiting my inward eye, and ear,
        With her gift of
Yowling exultation
        Would've been
Much noisier.

28 September 2020

The Shining City on the Hill

You see that Shining City on the Hill?
The shame is that the shine is just
The gleaming of the oily sheen
On the rats' backs swarming from its slums,
The shimmer of the stacks of trash,
The glister of the stolen gold
Reflected in the pools of blood,
The glistening of the sweat of slaves,
The sparkle of the film star's teeth,
The Milky Way of motes of stirred up dust
Twinkling in the beams that play around
The shadows as they tic across the cave,
The flicker in the polished dreams
Of Freedom, just a fresher theft
To free the thief to thieve, and thieve
Others' freedoms too, self-evidenced
By genocide and force transhumance
In a bolthole built for grifters
By bigots who sought havens for their hatreds,
And newly peopled by great waves of deadbeats
Who couldn't hack it in the Hapsburg Empire,
And dedicated to the proposition of straight teeth
For eating smaller dogs
While bombing and bamboozling the world
Into seeing it as advertised:
The Shining City on the Hill.

Though you know, don't you, that the shining's
Mostly just our shared sun (the patent's pending)
Setting through the smog. Right?

29 September 2020

Terf Wars

In diverting all our energies,
Each atom of our might and main,
To furiously fighting back against
Each slight and every hint of new injustice
With, every day, a fresh Thermopylae,
It's possible we may have missed the Gods
Of Greed and Pillage pointing out a path
High on the ledge, picked out among the rocks
Between bleached thorn bushes and crisp goat turds,
So now their full-blown Nazi furies
Have got us all encircled
      While we Spartans carry on
      Screaming at each other
      About how to comb our hair.

30 September 2020

Form and Content

Today is National Poetry Day, so I must now inform
The World that she whom I adore, she who keeps me warm,
Hates my verse, abhors my rhymes, thinks my scansion gorm-
Less. My love, alas, approves the content but deplores the form.

What I see as a refuge from the wild, encircling storm,
She sees as simply stinkier than a Belgian borstal dorm
And drippier than the rubber trees in a short story by Maugham.
Alas, my love approves the content but deplores the form.

It gets yet worse: not only does my verse underperform
Because it's written, so she claims, in ways outside the norm;
I think she thinks it should be eaten by a locust swarm.
My love, alas, approves the content but deplores the form.

Our daughter's worse, for she believes ALL poetry is grim;
Thinks trying to express your thoughts and feelings thus is lame,
Which leads me, with great sorrow, to conclude we must assume
She really hates the content AND truly deplores the form.

Me? I think that my poor verses have a certain chorm,
And by and large I kid myself that they do little horm.
Moreover they've a neutral impact on my huge incorm,
So I approve their content and I approve their form!

1 October 2020

The Crude but Catchy Victory Song of the Circling Viruses

Trump jumped!
Trump gazumped!
Trump stumped!
Trump rump pumped!
Frump chump Trump
Thumpingly humped!
Crumpled Trump
Dumped in a sump!
Mugwump Trump!
Trump trumped!
Trump jumped!
Trump gazumped!
Trump stumped!
Trump rump pumped!
Frump chump Trump
Thumpingly humped!
Crumpled Trump
Dumped in a sump!
Mugwump Trump!
Trump trumped!
Trump jumped!
Trump gazumped!
Trump stumped!
Trump rump pumped!
Frump chump Trump
Thumpingly humped!
Crumpled Trump
Dumped in a sump!
Mugwump Trump!
Trump trumped!

2 October 2020

Technical Errors

after Keats

Sea Sea Sea Sea
Season of mis...
Season of missssssssssss...
Season of mis – mis – mis – mis – mis
ED TARGETS MISSED OPPORTUNITIES MISSED DATA
Seaseaseaseaseaseaseaseas
Season Seasonnnnnnn
Seize on
ASYLUMSEEKERSASYLUMSEEKERSASYLUMSEEKERS
Seeeeeeeeeeeeeeezzzzzzzzz
NNnnnnnnnnnnnnggggggggg
Ooooooooooooooooooof
Mismismismismismismismis
ANTHROPIC FRUITLESSNESS
CLAUSTROPHOBIA OF A DWINDLING SUN
CONSPIRING WITH THEM HOW TO FUDGE THE MESS
WROUGHT FRUITILY BY PROUD THATCHERITE SCUM
See
   aaa
    sss
     o
      o
       o
       o
      o
     o
     o
      o
     o
    o

KLONK
Season of mists and mellow frightfulness
KONKONKONKONKONKONKONKONKONK
mmrrrrrrrrrrrrrrrrrrrrrrrrrrrrrrrrrrrrrrrrrrrrrrrrrrrrrrrrrrrrrrrrr
Thdok

5 October 2020

Full Recovery

Like the Minotaur
Once the ricks that formed
The Labyrinth's remit
At last rotted away
Crashing through and
Blinded by the sun
Thudding into the dust
Bellowing 'We've got this licked!'

Like the whale
Thumping up the beach
Air paddling its pectoral fins
Towards the dunes
While booming subsonically
'We'll beat this thing!',
Fine grains of sand
Rasping in its blowhole.

Like the elephant
That's suddenly in Outer Space,
Trying to trumpet
In the starlit silence
Of the total vacuum,
'Maybe now I'm immune, who knows?'
Giving a thumbless thumbs-up
In the nano-seconds prior to oblivion.

6 October 2020

Composed Upon Viewing the City of London from Blackfriars Bridge

after Wordsworth

Earth has not anything to show more crass:
Dullards rebuilt this mess with Duplo blocks,
Each twisted City skyscraper which mocks,
With ribs of steel and lungs of clouded glass,
Dissent from claims, that where there's muck, there's brass,
Where psychopaths sell other psychos' stocks
In spires designed by algorithms, a pox
That scars our cityscape, retold as farce,
And Crows' nests for the 27 Club –
And not those rock stars who od'd that age,
But 27 billionaires who rub
Soft hands while drooling like a coprophage
And own HALF the World's wealth. Beelzebub
Now glides between the towers, just to enrage.

8 October 2020

Eden

Some years ago George Monbiot
Told me his rewilding schemes,
Worthy and exquisite plans
For reconnecting rootless we
      With the Eden in us all,

With our internal wilderness
Caught inside, like Milton said,
And trapped in dreams or yearning hope,
But with his help we can break out
      Of our enclosed hearts.

And although Covid's done its best
To batter at the balustrades
Of human hubris, then as now
Nature still requires some help
      From her murderers' hands.

Enlightening landowners was,
He said, the way to dam against
The ecocidal flood now washing
Through the laceholes of our boots
      And corroding all our souls.

There was a problem though, he said.
The landowners all loved his schemes,
And saw them as a final chance
To clear out all their tenants so
      A hundred wastelands bloom.

Which goes to show that, while poor George
Rambles on the path to hell,
His knapsack spilling good intentions
Like breadcrumbs in the hungry woods,
      Eden's just bolus in the serpent's guts.

9 October 2020

Slogan

The kind of day
The work's so dull
The mind freefalls
      In Brownian motion
Ideas clump
Slogans cluster
Thoughts fandango
      Cascading through the mind
As you idly
Carve arabesques
On your femur
      With the point of your scythe
Nothing is good
Nothing is bad
Colon cancer's
      Just yesterday's beetroot
The tracheal
Haemorrhage is
Puked up red wine
      And coughs are simply coughs
Then the klaxons
Scream! Screens light up!
Back in action!
      The slogans spring to mind!
Adland copy!
Hookline sinkers!
'It ain't Covid
      Til the thin laddie swings!'

12 October 2020

Supporting the Arts

A nervous hollow knocking on the door
The Judas window rattles open.
Masked, in ragged motley, a dancer cringes
For a moment, retreating to the shadows,
Then edges forward, hunched, eyes darting,
Proceeding to perform a charmless caper,
Groaning throatily in self accompaniment.
Stale crusts are jettisoned through the snapping hatch,
Are grabbed in one thin hand, the other
Knuckling the cap and bells
Before they sidle jangling out of sight
To the adjoining cell there to reprise
The whole stupendous shtick.

And inside between the bars
A patch of sky can be beheld
Still grey and heavy with the never-ending downpour
Which soaked to sludge the flyer slipped
Beneath the door, where lichen spreads
Around the nailheads long since hammered
Into its frame, boasting about the goalers'
Continuing Investment in The Arts.

13 October 2020

Sovereign Vegetative State

Maybe it stops the screaming in his head,
Maybe it shows his mind is busy spooling Time
To back before his father broke his mother's nose
To wind things tight and leave no room
For confrontation or the need to make decisions.

Or maybe it's not screaming, but the absence of all sound,
The fearful silence where the laughter was,
When all difficulty's drowned out by the warmth of their guffaws,
Feeding off the energy of everyone's attention
In the internal realm of make-believe where that'll do instead of love.

Or maybe the constant flashes of pure panic in his eyes
Simply mean these days that the outside surrounding world's
Grown so filmed and blurry with the weight of consequence
All he can do is flip his gaze and peer at what's inside
Echo-locating futures charging roaring at another unlocked door
Into another empty, dusty room, its brown/green paint still flaking,
The only noise the hum of dodging molecules binding through sheer
                                                            boredom.

Which maybe makes him perfect, in this most terrible of times,
To lead our Sovereign Vegetative State,
A country in a cack-handed induced coma, strapped in yet more silence
Softly interrupted solely by the crass, regular pings of some machines
While the rest of us are butterflies, batting neverendingly
Against the gridded glass visages of an infinity
Of Diving Bells.

14 October 2020

Team Song

You put your tender in!
You drive your rivals out!
You send in your consultants
When the money's thrown about!
You put the Hokey-Covid
In your Turnover
        That's what it's all about!

Whooooaaaaaaa! Hokey-hokey-Covid!
Wheeeeeeeeeeee! Hokey-hokey-Covid!
Phwaaaoooooor! Hokey-hokey-Covid!
Knees bent
Boots filled
Ra-ra-ra!

You drive the numbers up!
You keep the proles locked down!
Send in more consultants
Who can go to town
Getting the Hokey-Covid
In our Turnover
        That's what it's all about!

Phwoooooaaaaaaar! Hokey-hokey-Covid!
Phheeeeeeeeeeeeew! Hokey-hokey-Covid!
Wheeeeeeeeeeeeeee! Hokey-hokey-Covid!
Lungs clogged
Boots filled
Ra-ra-ra!

We'll fuck up track and trace
But everything is fine!
The 'R' rate's on the rise
But so's the bottom line!
We've got the Hokey-Covid
In our Turnover
          That's what it's all about!

Seeeeeeeeeeeeeerco-key-hokey-Covid!
Diiiiiiiiiiiiiiiiiiiido-key-hokey-Covid!
Seeeeeeeeeeeeeerco-key-hokey-Covid!
Chums in
Boots filled
Ra-ra-ra!

15 October 2020

Covid Lit: Great Classics retold for Our Troubled Times

No 1: *Romeo & Juliet*

Two households both alike in dignity
Can only meet in groups of less than six,
In their own support bubble, not in their
Own homes, or outdoors, or in any public
Space, apart from indoors serving food, except
For emergency pubs, outdoors or indoors
On or in or under public transport. You,
Romeo, two metres away from that window.
End of.

15 October 2020

Poltergeist

In Lockdown 1 I thought, 'How nice
To get myself a poltergeist!
Some unquiet spook who'll bang and thump
And cheer us when we've got the hump,
Who'll make toothbrushes disappear
And lend this place some atmosphere,
A mischievously ghostly sprite
To give the girly swots a fright,
A clattering goblin from the grave –
You never got such larks with Dave!
Hearing bangs, some loud, some soft,
Echoing from the undercroft
Or from way up in the den
Right at the top of Number Ten
Where Geisty could thud with aplomb –
And be company for Dom!'
       But now we're in the Second Tier
My heart's begun to fill with fear.
You see, what started as a joke
Is no longer so okey-doke,
No longer such a wizard wheeze.
Instead a pall, like some disease,
Hangs in a mist throughout the place,
A presence beyond Time and Space,
A dank and damp eldritch miasma
That – O lawks – quite chills the plasma...
       And, for once, I won't dissemble.
The Cabinet no longer tremble
When Dom screams at some small error:
Instead they stare in abject terror
And Williamson voids his insides
When the table creaks and slides
Then melts and flops round like a squid
Then gells into a pyramid!
And Jacob, decked in crucifixes,

Pointedly no longer mixes
Afterwards, for tea and biccies.
The Civil Servants all pulled sickies
And Dom's weirdos and misfits, oddly,
Fled at first sight of The Ungodly.
      But worse yet is the deathly gloom
That suppurates through every room,
Beyond the nauseating feeling
As flocks of books swoop round the ceiling,
Knives and forks whizz through the air,
The carpets writhe above the stair,
The framed portrait of Bonar Law
Impales itself into the floor
And just now – Jesus! – Churchill's bust
Crumbled into seething dust
Which then reformed into a foetus
That hissed 'Give up! You'll never beat us!'
      And when they say I'm looking tired
They fail to understand I'm mired
Inside a hell I never chose!
I get no sleep! I barely doze!
I've tried counting me shagging sheep
But as I finally fall asleep
Another sudden thunderous thud
Forms ice crystals in my blood
And boiling hot, reason defied,
I'm bolt upright and wild, wide-eyed.
      Night after night, day after day!
At least C took that kid away,
But small relief brings no release!
It seems my torments will not cease!

Tried potions made from ash and jism,
Then I tried an exorcism,
Thrashed the air with bogbrush handles,
Muttered prayers by guttering candles,
But with each succeeding prayer
I'd lose another clump of hair
And hear, close by, a dreadful laugh.
Then blood began to fill the bath...
      And thuds and thumpings bang and clatter
O'er splats of ectoplasmic matter
And grunts and whines and cruel cackles
Make flesh creep on my rising hackles
BECAUSE I NEVER ASKED FOR THIS!
I was just taking the piss!
It was all a stupid lark!
The darkness darkens in the dark;
A clamminess consumes my skin;
Shame coughs up my every sin;
The remnants of my soul now slithers
From my nose. I'm chained in shivers
As things behind me start to moan,
Then bleeping from my mobile phone!
      A message! Trembling fingers grapple
To find what fresh torment a chap'll
Face now, what the Faustian pact
Has saved up for the final act...
      No earthly fears could ever presage
The dread I felt reading that message...

WE'RE NOT THROUGH YET – THERE'S LOADS MORE FUN
WE'LL SQUEEZE FROM YOU BEFORE YOU'RE DONE
AND SENT TO HELL – TO MAKE THINGS CLEAR
THERE'S 40,000 OF US HERE

20 October 2020

Poltergeist 2

Forgive me – be done in a trice,
But there's other kinds of poltergeist
Or, to be more imprecise,
A kind of noisy cockatrice
And servant of the Anti-Christ
Deployed to add a certain spice
To our affairs, there to entice
The gullible with merchandise
Invariably overpriced
While bellowing (yet quite concise)
That all our enemies are lice
And not as we are (we're like mice)
And thereby steep us in their vice
That equates hell with paradise
(Where all's seen as a game of dice
Through lying eyes, as chilled as ice)
Explaining how, when they top-slice,
It's their own brand of sacrifice.
Although, if you take my advice,
When watching these brash poltergeists
Slice and splice, once, twice, then thrice,
A single brittle grain of rice
And serve it up on edelweiss
Drawling 'All yours! Yum yum', suffice
It to say, the poltergeists
Make all that noise and come on nice
To blind you to their masters' heists.
Now that's me done on poltergeists.

21 October 2020

the rat report

after Don Marquis

to stop each other dying
they denied them all a life
so lived a kind of death
that was nothing close to living
except for those imposing what
they chose to choose to be
how the living
without a living
could only live by dying
because living is just buying anyway
though all of them were dying just
          to live

and what's that, ratlings?
you're asking what were these humans
actually good at? well, i suppose,
oh, jumping, jokes.
and genocide of course, the usual stuff
but nothing special

not that they thought so
though that was half the
problem
and honestly
i
wouldn't gnaw those bones
if i were
you

22 October 2020

Solipsism

Doubtless quite soon they'll calculate
That limited to meeting in
A simulacrum of The Real,
Some electronic Platospace,
People denied meeting their friends
And family and clearly see
The buggers stood across the room
Will then think no one else exists.

What we can't sense or smell or touch
Will ratchet back to broadcast lies,
A phoned face futilely fake news,
More bollocks from the Internet,
And this process of disbelief,
They'll calculate, the way they do,
Will take from nine months to a year
To achieve full Solipsism.

That said, such calculators flee
From rigour, as all humans must,
And make this shit up in their heads
Like philosophers long ago,
Their minds the perfect hermitage,
Their skulls the thickest prison walls,
An isolation hospital
For selfishness on cosmic scales.

Though far from us, the trees still flinch
In dank, unpeopled forest gloom,
Each time another loved one falls,
Unobserved by human pride,
And mighty oak trees mutely weep
In mourning for the broken ash
In their xylem and their phloem
That throb with tears rightly unheard

23 October 2020

The Clocks Go Back

The most magical season of the year
When Time itself rewinds,
All wrongs are wrangled and all regrets rowed back.

Except, of course,
The systems still in place
Will always let us down

So that, in practice,
In that special hour,
There can be no provision for the use of mobile phones

Or even email to inform
The denizens of all the threads and webs of twanged remorse
That processes are now in train to make things right once more.

And even if the landlines worked
It's 1am on Sunday morning, and everybody that you've hurt
Is either drunk or fast asleep.

And all preplanning, instrumental to
Turning Back The Clocks is, Chronologists insist, both
Unethical and way beyond the realms of Physics, as it's understood.

And as you've only got an hour which then, turned back, devours itself,
All constructs complex enough to make an ounce of difference to anything
Will always miss one last essential cog or wish and break as Time,
quite literally, runs out.

So you'll just have to wait again
Until the clocks go forward, and then try gathering into yet another hour
The boxes full of things you'd like to be deleted.

25 October 2020

Count Your Blessings!

Just consider, everybody knows how boring you've become,
Covid-19 is rife round here – you instantly succumb,
Your fingers, toes & arse & nose are worryingly numb,
You've just found out your fiancée is actually your mum,
The soup you sip served as the bath through which a rat has swum,
The silver foil around your bong's made of uranium,
You buccaneer the Spanish Main but are clean out of rum,
Your children simply won't leave home and leave it like a slum,
You hear the distant sound of Ed Sheerin begin to strum,
You feel your uncle's hand inside your jock-strap in the scrum,
You realise it's now been eleven years since you've come,
That flash of purest genius last night was *really* dumb,
Everything you touch turns into shit at once – ho hum,
You find in life's great lottery Piers Morgan's your best chum,
No figure in Greek Tragedy sank to the depths you plumb,
You recognise an ex-lover's tattoo on your new drum,
You wander past some roadkill and you drool out loud 'Yum yum!'
Your birthday cake's so foully baked you cannot eat a crumb,
Your boss started at primary school at the Millennium,
That's actually an Oxo cube and not some opium,
Your ex-spouse warns your kids about your equilibrium,
At La Scala, in your aria, you forget the words and hum,
There's a smell like rotting cabbage emanating from your thumb
And then, to cap it all, you've got a lobster up your bum...

But reflect, although you're wrecked, in one major respect,
However much you're stressed
Your life is truly blessed!
But how? I'm sure you've guessed:
You Are Not Tory Scum
Tory Scum
Tory Scum
Tory Scum
Tory Scum
Just thank Jesus Christ Almighty that you are not Tory Scum!

(Repeat forever)

25 October 2020

OD'd on Autumn

after Keats

Fusillades of rain roiling like airstrikes
Buzzed all night, just in earshot, like jarred flies;
Not caring if it ticks your likes or dislikes,
This season's eking out the summer's lies;
Cheap sunshine pimps dead leaves with an upgrade,
Old sentiment is spun from sniffed decay,
What's left of Nature's scuffed up like old leather
As night beats back the tired, depressive day,
Moves up the cordons, tightens the blockade,
Bolts doors and then breathes 'Join the masquerade!
Let's make believe it's such poetic weather!'

26 October 2020

Cultural Marxism

I met a Cultural Marxist
Who took me to *Swan Lake*
'Those swans denote the Class War!'
Quoth she. I found her take
Compelling if naive, but now
I'm told it's a disgrace
By a Cultural Fascist
Who then shot me in the face.

27 October 2020

Populism

You know the one!
　　　He's off the telly!
Does sidekick stuff! The light relief!
　　　And now he's giving proper wellie
To all those wokes who bring us grief.

Who do I mean?
　　　Well educated!
Goes on Twitter! Speaks his mind!
　　　His column's being syndicated.
He's got the common touch, you'll find.

Won't take it from
　　　No SJW!
Patriotic, not too grand
　　　He'll back you should a leftie trouble you
And now he needs a helping hand.

A brand new party!
　　　Proper backing!
From hedgies just like you and me
　　　To help him send the woke scum packing
And help to set the people free!

He's off the telly!
　　　He's proper famous!
He's also got a famous dad!
　　　And yes, he'd now like to retain us...
Come on! He did that teabag ad!

You must know him!
　　　This is too much!
He's famous! He's been on TV!
　　　He's posh but got the common touch,
Plus, he is his own chimpanzee!

Did the teabags!
Does loud hooting!
Really apey! Really rocks!
The ape bit might affect recruiting?
All right then! We'll use Laurence Fox...

28 October 2020

Church and State

Wafting tufts of burning ermine,
A shower of shards of chipped gold paint.
No coach could handle that sharp turning
On the road to meet the saint.

The saint squats, miles beyond the blackspot,
In a hermitage of bones,
Metal sheets, planks pocked with wet rot,
Flapping prayer flags, mobile phones.

The coach, heart of the grand procession,
Had been packed full of dynamite
To guard the monarch with discretion
From any little oversight.

Perhaps the watching, cheering peasants
Might yearn to seek the monarch's grace
And storm the coach! The monarch presence
Now constituted half a face.

Nor were there any peasants cheering.
The recent plague had seen them off.
Though in a nearby forest clearing
Five huddled, trying not to cough.

The coach careened as it had cornered
And tipped exploding down the gulch.
Regal scraps rained; local fauna'd
Browsed upon the royal mulch.

The carts behind the coach had splintered
And the monarch's retinue,
With whom the monarch overwintered,
Became a gory curlicue.

The pilgrimage to seek out saintly
Intercession with a miracle
Had been the monarch's idea, quaintly,
To defy the dark empirical

The plan had left the courtiers quizzical:
The nation could be saved through prayer?
The monarch was now metaphysical,
Smithereened into the air.

The saint ignored the monarch's lateness
And chewed upon a soggy frond
Meditating on the greatness
Of the infinite beyond

And soon was quite obscured by drizzle
Which washed away the monarch's sins,
Not knowing if to laugh or grizzle,
Each separate as conjoined twins.

29 October 2020

Scarred Borough Fare

Are we going to fuck it all up?
Ignore SAGE, raise 'R' all the time?
We've nailed the northerners inside their slums
But once those idiots voted for us!

30 October 2020

The Migrants

In the hot stiffling tiny room
The cold dead eyes blanked
            Even an iota
Of their torment or their tears
Or their mourning as the dead voice
            Catechized on quotas,
Spoke flatly of the processes,
Rules, restrictions, retributions,
            The penalties compounded by each error,
The limits on their movements,
The denial of information,
            The incremental, automatic ratchetting of terror
Until, right at the end,
The mask slipped for an instant
            As they stood to be led out and their feet began to burn:
The demon scratched its horns and shrugged
And mumbled, 'I just don't get it.
            When will these klutzes ever learn?
Why do they keep on coming here at all?
Ah well. Funny old world.' The demon coughed into the sulphurous
            Air and picked up a pile of ledgers
As on the wall behind it
The current Hell Secretary's portrait
            Got crispier at its edges
While they were led away
To a distant pit, to wait. And wait. And wait
            And wait among rank upon innumerable rank
Of those who'd made it this far,
Far further than the corpses washing through the clinker
            And clumped along the Styx's opposite bank.

30 October 2020

The New Jerusalem

The tattered flag snaps in the gale.
The old man pouts; looks out to sea
To where, without the Tide's betrayal,
The New Jerusalem should be.

30 October 2020

Late, Later, Latest, Last Capitalism

All Life on Earth
Is overvalued;
Offers
Diminishing
Returns

Whereas the Formless
Timeless Void
Of Utter
Non-existent
Nothingness
        Futures
Are already performing strongly
In early trading as Wall Street readies
        To yawn open.

2 November 2020

The Boiling Lake

Across the placid surface of the boiling lake
Is spread a thin meniscus, a flimsy film,
More sheer than late Spring ice, and which is constantly
Dissolving, melting or evaporating just behind you,
Compelling you to move towards the distant shore,
Tight-roping on these fine yet thicker veins, the scars of former fissures.

Only almost in earshot, in the corner of your eye,
The boiling lake is variously discharged,
Its roiling waters roaring through the turbines of twelve dams,
Each named after a virtue as defined by its constructors:
'Wealth', 'Punishment', 'Obedience' – you get the point.
Their watchtowers seem spindly through the mounds of crashing spray.

And skimming, sliding, skating, stumbling or skidding across the lake
You can glance down crystal clearly into its churning depths
Where hulking, looming things embroil themselves in orgies of destruction.
Some intermittently float up to batter at you right beneath your feet,
Regular nearby rending noises alerting you to others, just like you,
Going under through a fissure, in a final, tiny blur of red and blue.

Yet you tiptoe on, only microns from the maelstrom's careless indifference,
Still safe, right at this moment, closer to the distant dark and sunlit shore,
And there isn't any other lake, there are no landscapes
Conceivable, constructable, feasible beyond what's here,
Ameliorated, nonetheless, by amalgamated acts of random kindness
So, laughing with exhilaration and loving every second you've got left,
    you race on.

3 November 2020

THE BOILING LAKE

The Kind Anthropologist

Turkey vultures are still roosting there beneath the broken dome
And the shaman shuffles once again across the dusty ground
Arranging rows of old tin cans, each one representative
Of a former state and into each of which he starts to drop
With jerky deliberation, from his shrivelled, filthy mouth
Sucked m&ms, lilac and pink, guided by the ritual,
Slyly slugging dark brown hooch with every freshly filled mouthful
From a dirty jam jar that he keeps behind the altar stone,
Before which now the children, pimped in tattered fancy dress,
Move round and round in a lacklustre dance, their sullen chanting
Quite imperceptible above the rustling of the vultures
Who yawn, primping their feathers. The shaman starts to ululate
And hops from foot to foot and shakes a broken old broom handle
Wrapped around in silver tinsel and scratched with simple symbols,
    The meaning of which even he's forgotten.

The Kind Anthropologist is jolted from her daydreams
By her assistant's sudden snore, so elbows him to wake him
As the whole performance has been staged entirely just for them
Plus the benefit of Science so she hisses in his ear:
"We're almost at the part when the children get to kill the duck!"
She smiles at the filthy brats now lining up beneath the shrine,
An old, ruined edifice of rubble, straw and plastic bags.
And even though, in broken badlands way beyond the beltway
In pockets of tribal settlements pocked across the prairie
They whore after their different gods, she still feigns fascination
For these strange old traditions, and despite the screaming boredom
On the faces of the children now handed cutthroat razors,
She blinks politely when she takes the duck's still warm, downy head
From the gnarled, dirty fingers of the gap toothed, gurning shaman
    As furtively she starts chewing on khat.

4 November 2020

The Elephant in the Room: At the Commencement of the Latest Lockdown

The elephant that's in this room
   Just shat upon the floor.
I know what everybody says;
   They say – simply ignore!
But when the bastard's shat again
No self-respecting chatelaine
   Could cope with it much longer. Furthermore

That elephant's been in this room since,
   Let's see, well before,
The end of March, and just slouched round
   To block the exit door!
And now he gone and shat again!
Over my Persian mat! Explain
   How we endure this for a month! Before

The latest rules I tried to tie
   A face mask to his trunk.
He lifted his enormous leg
   And showered me with spunk,
And now the fucker's shat again!
He's on some fucking scat campaign!
   The worst of it's I can't even get drunk.

That's because all of the booze
   Long since went up his trunk.
Plus he's scoffed all of the biscuits,
   Though there's nowt in which to dunk
And – Jesus Christ – he's shat again!
And tough if you find that profane,
   Because the cunt's just shat another hunk!

Stuck with each other in this tiny room
   We two shall skulk.
I'll try and finish off this verse
   And he, no doubt, will sulk.
And obviously he's shat again.
Torment like this would twat Verlaine.
   Very soon I hope that he will crush me with his bulk.

The alternative is paddling in his poop,
   Spread through the room,
Though what the creature symbolises
   I dare not to presume.
I'll just observe, he's shat again.
I think you might find that germane
   As we glower at each other, left together in this tomb.

5 November 2020

The Elephant in the Room

Maxine's Vaccine

Maxine? Maxine! Maxine? Maxine!
You. Won't. Be. Getting. That. Vaccine.
From reading the Dark Web I glean
It's made from kiddies Charlie Sheen
Has processed through a huge machine
And laced with polypropylene
That acts like nitroglycerin
When ingested! Turns your spleen
Orange, then ultra-marine!

Maxine? Maxine, Maxine, Maxine!
It's deadlier than a guillotine!
They tested it on wolverine!
It cancels out your dopamine
And makes you bend like Plasticine
To their will! It's quite obscene!
And when they say it's just routine,
You think they tell the truth? Maxine!
When were you born! Where have you been?

Oh yes, they call it "quarantine",
But only so that they can screen
The old to make more Soylent Green!
It's the Elite! They're like gangrene!
All went to Eton or Roedean!
Out of their skulls on Benzadrine!
Panels of "experts" who convene
With masonic Jews...
                        ...Maxine?
Come back Maxine! I didn't mean...!

Maxine? Maxine? Maxine? Maxine!
THINK OF HER MAJESTY THE QUEEN!!
Oh let her go. I won't demean
Myself by grovelling to a teen.
She's made her own bed, has Maxine,
And I bet those sheets aren't clean,
All smeared with things like vaseline.
And nobody has even seen
This so-called virus! Call me green
But next up they'll ban Ovaltine!
MAXINE! MAXINE! MAXINE! MAXINE!
Don't you be getting that vaccine.

10 November 2020

Armistice Day

Six whole months ago today
I opened up a Second Front
All of my own, my little war
To bear witness and raise morale
Through tiny actions, slogans daubed
On to a burned-out outhouse wall,
Seditious homilies on cards
Inserted into library books,
And hieroglyphs stencilled beneath
The moon's face, masked with fleeting clouds,
Over another poster of some square-jawed heroine.

And who knows? I may graduate
To cutting the telegraph wires,
Blowing up overgrown branch lines,
Taking potshots at a general
Sipping pastis in a café
But merely singe the epaulettes
Of one of his young aides-de-camp.

Although my co-conspirator
Had disappeared after day one,
Either shot or conscripted by
One of the several ignorant
Armies that get crass each night,
Or scarecrowed on the barbed wire like
A pallid Wykehamist poet,
Or fled through furtive channels to
Drink absinthe through the afternoon
Outside squalid bars in Irun,
Or turning tricks in Lisbon and
Insanely imagining that
Tomorrow there will be a berth
Towards a Brave New World.

But still, today's Armistice Day,
The day they say the guns fall quiet,
Although the dead keep mounting up,
The refugees cower in their camps,
Boarded up in bomb-proof shelters,
Huddling in a fresh shell crater
While rumours multiply like lice,
Of traitors, tyrants, potions or
Of secret weapons, great new breakthroughs,
Final outcomes, Victory at last...
Though over what remains unclear:
The war aims remain to pursue
The War Aims. For King and Empire,
Queen and Country, or whatever
Construct now pertains for that old
Quagmire, moating a mud island
Covered with stockades of donkeys
All of an ancient pedigree
Braying, like they always have, long
Into the crackling night beside
Full mangers made of solid gold.

But even if the Armistice
Should turn out to be real, and holds,
Despite all previous ceasefires being broken
With all the martial rallying cries
More stinking wasted breath as more
Fresh corpses give up further ghosts;
But even if it holds, what then?

If you've caught the cut of Armistices' jibs
You already should know what's coming next:
After the emperors' tumblings, then the coups,
Then the final clenched-teeth admission that
Futility is the least of war's flaws,
The Peace Conference, the bragging revenge,
The brutal reparations, how they'll bodge
Reimposing pre-War status quos,
The civil wars, the famines, revolutions,
The unemployment, the hunger marches,
The hollow hopelessness of promises
Of a land fit for heroes anyone
Could then look in the eye and not feel shame,
The lock-outs, means tests, shack towns, bread lines, wars,
The bank runs, market crashes, then the Nazis
    And the re-run, and the
    Re-run after that,
And never ever closer to the cracked
And sun-bleached uplands in the bleary distance.

So all in all hug this war close
In case it wrestles free to run
Capering away, laughing at
The looks upon our faces.

And me? I'm working up to digging trenches.

11 November 2020

Burial

Pepys buried a Parmesan
   During the Great Fire
But what would you elect to save
   From Fate's Capricious Ire?

Rosetti buried poetry;
   Dean Swift? A Houyhnhnm!
Dylan Thomas, twenty pints of beer
   Full up to the brim!

The Pharoahs buried wives and slaves
   And cats and grain and gold;
The wary bury diaries full of tales
   Not to be told.

A pirate buries treasure;
   A squirrel buries nuts;
Speculators bury surpluses
   To see them through the gluts.

What should you save by burying?
   A book? Some wine? A glove?
Your passport, or a locket
   Of the one you truly love?

Some hair from your first baby?
   Your old dad's broken pipe?
The clutter of a lifetime,
   Or your life until it's ripe?

And what does Boris Johnson love,
   He buries and he saves?
Why! 50,000 citizens
   Now buried in their graves.

12 November 2020

Beethoven's Fifth

Dom Dom
  is gone
Dom Dom
  Is gone
Dom Dom Dom Dom
Dom Dom Dom Dom
Dom Dom Dom Dom
Dom Dom
  Is gone
To play Minecraft under
Michael Gove's bed
  And recount the moon,
While in his mind his enemies
Are crushed by great machines.
  Bless.

14 November 2020

Obsessional

after Kipling

The oddballs & misfits depart
All futurecasters exeunt
The briefings drift off like a fart
The whole thing just a childish stunt
Dom Going's revealed as, at heart,
A wanker – not even a cunt.
Lest we forget – and let's be blunt:
A wanker. Not even a cunt.

15 November 2020

Leprosia

As the trade talks recommenced
The leper leader, in his shack
Alone, was too consumed with languor
To brush the flies from off his eyes.

The envoy from Leprosia
(The free colony's new name)
Sat opposite his counterpart,
Across a broad and flaking table.

The Isolation Hospital's
Negotiator, in the torpor,
Squinted at the ceiling's glare
Reflected from the dusty yard.

Flies resting on the fan's blades
Observed in fractals compromises
Over morgue and graveyard access
Conceded morosely.

Then, at last, a vague conclusion,
Just firm enough to hold til dusk.
The Hospital's envoy joked
'We're now called Consumptia!'

His laugh became a coughing fit.
He screwed his hankie in his pocket,
Thumbing some dampness on his cuff.
All thought it best not to shake hands.

16 November 2020

Shakespearean Tragedy

They've painted King Lear Orange!
He's mad as mad can be!
Divides the state! Will Ivanka
Be given Tennessee?

They've painted Hamlet Orange!
Does that arras hide Pence?
Does Dad still haunt? Melania!
Get to a nunnery hence!

Othello too is Orange!
With Green Eyed Monster pout
Paranoia drives him mad!
Melania! Watch out!

They've painted King Lear Orange!
On and on he rages!
I know this is Shakespearean
But it goes on for ages!

They painted Hamlet Orange!
To quit or not to quit
Has never even crossed his mind.
This soliloquy's shit!

Now Caesar's also Orange!
Though stabbed any amount
He yells at the conspirators
'Fake News! Recount! Recount!'

And King Lear is still Orange
Beneath the roaring sky!
It's Tragedy, so let's assume
Eventually he'll die.

Although Hamlet's still Orange!
And still he won't decide!
But Christ! This is a Tragedy!
Isn't it time he died?

Falstaff, Prince Hal, Mark Antony!
All Orange too! What class!
But though we all love Tragedy
Being replayed as Farce

Paint no more heroes Orange:
Such work need not detain us.
Just drop the first three syllables
From off 'Coriolanus'.

17 November 2020

The Public School Ethos

Do Etonians eat onions
       With a Georgian silver spoon?
Do Harrovians drive horror vans
       Beneath a blood red moon?
Are all Alleynians aliens,
       Green Martians neath the skin?
Do Wykehamists hold wiccan rites
       And sacrifice their kin?
Are Carthusians Cartesians,
       Just dualistic boobs?
And do Salopians hatch from eggs
       And not fallopian tubes?
Do Roedeanians ride on
       Rhodesian ridgebacks?
Have any of these brats suffered
       From physical attacks?
Do Marlburians smoke Malboros?
       Are Stoics stoic? (Yes I know,
But this is what they call those sods
       Who went to school at Stowe)
And do Fettesians fetishise
       How fitting is the fate
Of children who are taught to think
       They're smart, and good, and great?
But eliminate alumni
       And I'm told you'll find the jobs
The nation needs done urgently
       Will all be done by yobs,
Unschooled and undependable,
       And simply the wrong tool
To sort out track and trace or PPE,
       And why? Wrong school!

But if you ask a favour
        From a nice Public School kid
There's every chance they'll do it
        For under a million quid!

18 November 2020

Normal Christmas

after Sammy Cahn & Jule Styne

The World outside is frightening,
But you might get struck by lightning
Don't wanna spend Xmas in bed
Let it spread let it spread let it spread!

The smiles on the kiddies' faces
As nobody tracks and traces
And Gran and her carer are dead
Let it spread let it spread let it spread!

We tried out herd imm-un-ity
And snogged neath the mistletoe
Decimating our comm-un-ity
And now it won't even snow!

This year we've no tree – we're spruceless
And the Government is useless,
These leaders are as toxic as lead
Let it spread let it spread let it spread

And because he's stuck in lockdown
Santa's not on his way
So we've started knocking the hock down
By drinking til Boxing day!

And though we'll try to feel perky
We've all been stuffed like turkeys
But without the Brussels! So, unfed,
Let it spread left it spread let it spread!

19 November 2020

Lost

I

Last night I heard on Radio 4
The man who's won the Booker Prize
Be asked a questioned which contained
The phrase 'you lost your mother...'

I didn't lose mine. She lost me,
Left me for someone else to find
Then moved away. My next mother
Lost me as well, repeatedly.

Or more exactly, she'd flaneur
With us in front, to keep an eye
On us until a shop window
Caught it instead, while on we walked

And then once more I'd find myself
In a kind policeman's arms
Him laughing and her cross, exposed,
I now suppose, as careless.

My father lost things all the time.
I'd help find them. He never lost
His wife and natural child: they died.
We knew precisely where they were.

In morgues. Then coffined. Then in flames.
Then in the ground. And if you like
I can pinpoint the exact spot
They share now with my father.

II

Yet in that expanding lexicon
Of words we need to leave unsaid,
We seem to think, to mutter 'die'
Somehow invokes and summons Death

And so instead, we're lost or pass,
Like umbrellas or passing thoughts,
Or, for that matter, water (though
In this case what we mean is piss)

Because we're all so childish
A harsh word might scare us to death.
Or to pass. Better, get lost,
Just loose change dropped down the settee.

III

Then I remembered I'd forgot
To wheel the bins out in the street.
The instant I stepped through the door
November enveloped me

Its coldness grabbing down my throat,
Its dampness oozing like a sponge
Its perfumes rich, redemptive death
In leaf mould, coal smoke, burning wood

The evening was a slap of joy
The kind that makes you gulp first breaths
And breathe and breathe until you're done
The senseless scents of Rex Mundi

The whole Autumn accreted fresh
Layers onto Death's millefeuille
Each death podsolled and swaddling
The next arriving layer of Life.

So maybe we can't say the name
The same way that you don't feel wet
Fully immersed in water as
We all pass through, before we're lost.

Invigorated, my old heart
Started to sing in inner realms
Where, once you just start to look,
In the end you'll find it all.

20 November 2020

The Twenty-Second of November

On St Cecilia's Day they change the tunes
Pumped into the waiting rooms
Of Purgatory
Where Aldous Huxley, C.S. Lewis and
John Fitzgerald Kennedy
Are sat side by side
United in their date of death. Each tics
An instant as the music
Stops, and then plays on.
Lewis chews his lower lip, still rattled
By Eternity's delays
Granting Salvation
Gnawed by spasms of unclear remorse
After a wingless angel
Showed him his chair and
Said 'It's just a thing with 'The Last Battle'.
No need for you to worry,
I'm sure. Please wait here.'
Jack Kennedy pays him no attention
Continuing to toss nuts
Into the air and
Then try catching them in his skull's chasm.
Huxley shudders, guessing it's
An acid flashback.

Far below, Margaret Thatcher too
Observes the music changing.
That's another year
Since she resigned and then started to die.
But there's no time to ponder,
Pause and then reflect.
The fixed conditions of her damnation
Require that she dance tangos
For the Rest of Time
With A.E. Housman, across crusty floors
Of their designated pit
In Hell, reserved for
Those Cursed Souls Who Have Quite Fucked Up England
Infusing her with fatal
Enthusiasms,
Mawkish Deathcults, Tight-arsed Nature Worship
And Small Town Cold Hearts.
Their faces turned eternally away
From each other's gaze, each hear
Through 4000 miles
Of clenching granite, England still whining
Through unending peevish pouts
Above the noise of
Chainsaws play 'A Walk In The Black Forest'
Over and over again
On St Cecilia's Day.

22 November 2020

The Flitting Muse

My Muse flits like a startled faun,
Tossing her noble head.
Cries out 'We're through!' Can it be true
I've said all to be said?

She'd earlier binned her laurels, taken
Up a thorny crown,
More of the bint's unsubtle hints
Just trying to get me down.

At parties she would roll her eyes,
Spurn an Ambrosial snack,
Abjure a glass of Nectar, pass
Instead to smoking crack

She'd pout as we crashed book launches,
Get stuck into the drink,
Flirt, as a tease, with enemies,
Then vomit in a sink

Sneer at my toga as we'd waft
Through an Elysian grove,
Then slap cheese into tapestries
Which we together wove

Read out my verses mockingly, while
Plucking at a lyre
Then feed my scrolls throughout the hols
Onto a summer fire

And now she's gone, gone with our owl,
Both hooting with derision.
Taken her chariot to a Marriott.
I honour her decision.

But shall her curses spoil my verses
Abandoned now by Muses?
On this boy plods! I beg to gods
To free me from these floozies!

I'll sacrifice a goat tonight so
My verse won't get ropier!
Her victory's Pyrrhic! I'll tease the Lyric
From my Cornucopia!

I won't repine! Circean swine
Could not give me the blues!
Tore my raiment, made a down payment
On a mail order Muse.

24 November 2020

The Curtain

Does everybody get that thing?
Clench the eyes tight shut
And start to see, not in the mind,
But truly see,
A vortexing kaleidoscope of tiny sepia
And burnt umber squares and stars and rhomboids
Palladianing down a tunnel whose fixed point of exit
Lies at the dead centre of
The whole field of non-vision?

For decades I imagined that
This tenebrous firework display, although
A thing, an aspect of palpable reality
And not simply the ragged scrap of a dream's edge that
Had poked through from deeper expanses of my clear and hidden
                                                    thinking,
That this must be something between
A glimpse of the atomic structure lying in wait in everything
And some sort of membrane that divides
Internal from external worlds.

It turns out that I'm wrong on both those counts.
These lights are called phosphenes, and what one sees –
Or what I see, because these words
Might sound like mad Sanskrit screamed
Into a cushion to anybody else but me –
Is simply the vestigial light remaining
In my eyeballs, still compelled to bounce against
Their rods and cones and rendered into sparks my brain
Displays as dirty stars and suns in the total darkness.

It doesn't really matter either way
Even if, deep from back inside early childhood nights,
I've liked imagining the swirling lightshow is a curtain
I can twitch and thus check out what's up on either side,
Particularly this year, this sabbatical from ecocide,
This failed correction, one more flawed exercise
In albeit brutal biocontrol, though now,
Accompanied by a crescendo of deadly Doppler chords of clawing back
normality
The Juggernaut slips with a crunch of bones back in to gear

And on we blithely writhe, hang out the torn-up shrouds as bunting
In a fresh fiesta for the Heist Christ, still led on by bumptious, loud class
clowns
Whose names grace blistering boards in old school halls and, if they're
blessed,
One day a cracking cul de sac that leads to bricked up depots full of loot
Between catacombs of bedsits, where petrifying certainties sedimenting
in their skulls
Squeeze people's minds out through blocked ears to sizzle for a second
As opinions pass for politics and tantrums for debate
With extermination for dissent remaining a distinct option
As they plop onto the curling lino.

For over half a year I've Cartier-Bressoned all of that,
Strait-jacketing my instant take, like this, both in and out.
All that unstinting witnessing, of Death, cranked cranks, the crooks and
all that
Embarrassingly gauche gratitude for just the meagrest dollop of what's-
next-might-not-be-quite-so-bad
Reminds me to get back inside and hunker round the richly glowing
embers
And watch you smile, then look down to the knitting on your lap,
And laugh. That does for now, forever, so I'm drawing back the curtain
And ignoring for a bit the killing constantly begetting killing. Though
remember:
However much you hate them, viruses are people too.

25 November 2020

The Banquet

The bankers and the viruses
        Arranged to have a dinner
Where the viruses looked tired
        And the bankers slightly thinner.
The viruses proposed a toast:
        'Chaos! And Bonhomie!
To our eternal bond in
        Crashing the Economy!'

The bankers bridled. Several laughed.
        A fat one drawled: 'Pur-leeeze!
We're the Engines of Prosperity!
        And you're just a disease!
And we're nothing like you!
        This comparison's obscene!
And we'll prove it by investing
        To create a new vaccine!'

'Speaking,' the viruses replied,
        'As disease to disease,
There's no need to display your guilt-
        Edged insecurities!
Be proud of your achievements
        And how you make your cash!
We've loved '08 and '29
        And every other Crash!

'True, you could be more proactive;
        Fewer sins of omission,
But you make up for that with the
        Monstrous size of your commission!
It's just you lack all agency,
        Just do what bankers do,
Which lacks the subtle beauty
        Of a nasty bout of flu!

But still, your avarice and greed,
        Like our infectious ways
Have thankfully hastened mankind
        Towards the End of Days!
With poverty and misery
        And all kinds of how d'you do!
Eventually we'll kill them off
        Together! Cheers! Salut!'

The bankers rose in fury
        At the speaking of this libel;
Respectable and titled, they flung
        'Who's Who' like a bible!
Screamed 'We will make a vaccine
        That will see you commies off!'
But in their midst a banker
        At this point began to cough.

You remember that scene near the end
        Of *Raiders of the Lost Ark*?
Like that, but as to details
        I shall leave you in the dark.
Many of those bankers died,
        Others were very ill.
The viruses then did the decent thing
        And paid the bill.

26 November 2020